The Puffin

AN INSIDER'S GUIDE TO
CREATIVE WRITING
PROGRAMS

Brown U.
Loyola Marymount U. (LA)
U. of Texas-Austin

AN INSIDER'S GUIDE TO
CREATIVE WRITING
PROGRAMS

Amy Holman

PRENTICE HALL PRESS

THE BERKLEY PUBLISHING GROUP
Published by the Penguin Group
Penguin Group (USA) Inc.
375 Hudson Street, New York, New York 10014, USA
Penguin Group (Canada), 90 Eglinton Avenue East, Suite 700, Toronto, Ontario M4P 2Y3, Canada (a division of Pearson Penguin Canada Inc.)
Penguin Books Ltd., 80 Strand, London WC2R 0RL, England
Penguin Group Ireland, 25 St. Stephen's Green, Dublin 2, Ireland (a division of Penguin Books Ltd.)
Penguin Group (Australia), 250 Camberwell Road, Camberwell, Victoria 3124, Australia (a division of Pearson Australia Group Pty. Ltd.)
Penguin Books India Pvt. Ltd., 11 Community Centre, Panchsheel Park, New Delhi—110 017, India
Penguin Group (NZ), cnr. Airborne and Rosedale Roads, Albany, Auckland 1310, New Zealand (a division of Pearson New Zealand Ltd.)
Penguin Books (South Africa) (Pty.) Ltd., 24 Sturdee Avenue, Rosebank, Johannesburg 2196, South Africa

Penguin Books Ltd., Registered Offices: 80 Strand, London WC2R 0RL, England

This is an original publication.

Copyright © 2006 by Amy Holman
Text design by Stacy Irwin
Cover design by Liz Sheehan

PRINTING HISTORY
Prentice Hall Press trade paperback edition / May 2006

Prentice Hall Press is a registered trademark of Penguin Group (USA) Inc.

ISBN: 0-7352-0405-5

This book has been cataloged by the Library of Congress

PRINTED IN THE UNITED STATES OF AMERICA

10   9   8   7   6   5   4   3   2   1

ACKNOWLEDGMENTS

A book of this scope cannot be attempted without a dialogue with the writing public and the organizations and foundations that serve its needs. For nineteen years, I joined this community through my positions at the national nonprofit, Poets & Writers, Inc., and I am very grateful to all the writers who sought me out for answers to how they could improve their writing and support their careers. As well, I am indebted to the Associated Writers and Writing Programs (AWP), P.E.N. American Center, The Foundation Center, Alliance for Artist Communities, and Res Artis.

Over the years I have listened to writers speak of their experiences with graduate programs, artists colonies, grants, and fellowships. But, I especially wish to thank Janice Eidus, Denise Duhamel, Nick Carbó, Leslie Shipman, Mia Anderson and Kamal Ayyildiz for their answers to my particular questions.

The enthusiasm and flexibility of my agent, Elisabeth Weed, was second only to her support of my book, whatever outfit it chose to wear. And my gratitude extends to the vision and encouragement of my editor, Marian Lizzi, who let this book be.

CONTENTS

INTRODUCTION

Every successful writer has the time to write, a suitable environment to set the muses free, and money to support this reflective art. In short, the author has permission to sit in a room for hours and scribble her way into literature. Without permission, there's no focus; without focus, there's no writing; without completed works, there's no income from writing. But finding focus in a busy life or at a time of transition is not as easy as we wish it is, and often we grant ourselves permission only after others have authorized us to continue our stories, poetry, essays, plays, or novels through praise, encouragement, acceptance, or publication.

But beyond our friends or editors at magazines and publishing houses, there are institutions, organizations, and foundations that offer the biggest encouragement and permission of all. *An Insider's Guide to Creative Writing Programs* delivers to you 153 graduate creative writing programs (60 detailed in the book; all 153 listed on the

CD-ROM), 81 Colonies and Residencies in the United States and abroad (47 detailed in the book; all 81 listed on the CD-ROM), and 74 grants and fellowships (26 detailed in the book; all 74 listed on the CD-ROM). Any of these opportunities permit you to write, advance your career, and expand your vision as a literary artist.

The CD-ROM has links to the websites (or e-mail addresses if no website exists) to all the listings in this book and to programs not listed. I suggest you follow my lead in researching graduate programs, colonies, residencies, grants, and fellowships and consider all the attributes of each. Many graduate writing programs have options of applying online and many colony and grant applications can be downloaded. The CD-ROM is searchable by genre, state, country, and where applicable, degree offered and type of program.

A few notes about the scope and emphasis of this book: This guide covers full-on **graduate writing programs,** most of which are Masters in Fine Arts, and some of which are Masters of Arts. It does not include the myriad programs in English with emphasis, concentration, or option in creative writing. In terms of **artists and writers colonies** and **residency programs,** the book focuses on those that do not require payment, aside from purchasing one's own food to cook or travel arrangements. However, some of the hybrid colonies that accept a writer based on the merit of his or her work but require payment to stay are included on the CD-ROM under "Other Opportunities." This book covers **grants** and **fellowships,** sometimes called **awards** and **prizes,** for writing and for specific projects to which you can apply, not those for which you can be nominated. It does not include contests, prizes, and awards for individual works or books to be published, or for books already published. This book also does not cover writers conferences, festivals, and retreats, which are other great—but different—opportunities.

And while I've got you on the same page, let me warn you about the appropriation of language, and how to best understand the opportunities listed in this book. First, the title of my book expands the definition of *programs* to include opportunities that are not, by strict definition, including grants and colonies. *Artist* sometimes includes literary artists or writers. Colonies have residents they sometimes call *fellows*, and some colonies refer to themselves as *residency programs* even though they do not require the resident writers to give back to the community. The artist-in-residence and writer-in-residence programs do require the writer to teach, give a presentation, and, in some instances, donate work. And this use of residence has nothing to do with the graduate writing programs, which require the students who have been accepted into the program and paid tuition to be in attendance at the university, residing on- or off-campus for the duration of a regular program, or for eight to ten days out of each semester for the low-residency program. These distinctions will be made clear in each section of this book.

An Insider's Guide to Creative Writing Programs makes a case for all of these programs, yet distinguishes for you if, when, and why you would want to pursue them, and how—but not exactly in that order. Throughout the individual lists are quotes from writers who have attended these places, describing what their experiences were like and what the programs enabled them to do. My intent is to open your minds to possibilities you might have overlooked, thought were closed to you, or worried were too hard to pursue, and to change your mind about them.

So go ahead and turn the page to explore the creative writing programs that await you. I am here to help you make the right decisions to move forward in your writing career and find continued success.

1 **The Opportunities Await You**

Choosing the Right Program at the Right Time

The opportunities in this book ideally span an entire writing career, from MFA degree to NEA grant, although no one writer needs to participate in all three areas to have a successful career. The writer who is a student of a graduate writing program will not be eligible to apply for grants, fellowships, colonies, or residencies until his or her degree is achieved. After that, the field is fairly open to you, with some exceptions. In general, if you can be accepted into an artists colony, or for residency in a park, community center, or school, then you can also get a state arts grant. Overseas colonies often require writers to be more accomplished before they apply, and many foundations require writers to have a publication history before they will grant them a fellowship. Even if you think that you need this book only for Chapters 4 and 5, let me say that the more you build your résumé with published books, colony residencies, and fellowship wins, the better chances you have at becoming a visiting writer at a resident writing program or guest faculty at a low-residency program. So keep that list of programs in Chapter 3 close at hand.

■ A LITTLE HISTORY . . .

Granting writers permission to create was in the collective unconscious in the beginning of the twentieth century, and once the windows began opening, so did the doors. Katrina Trask may have had a vision in the late 1880s of artists, composers, and writers wandering her estate in Saratoga Springs, New York, "creating, creating, creating," but family tragedy derailed the opening of Yaddo until four years after her death in 1926, which means that the founding in 1907 of The MacDowell Colony in Peterborough, New Hampshire, made it the first artists colony. It opened its little cottage doors in 1908, around the time The Byrdcliffe Colony in Woodstock, New York, established its largely arts-and-crafts colony that nevertheless hosted the young poet Wallace Stevens. In 1925, Senator and Mrs. Simon Guggenheim founded The John Simon Guggenheim Foundation in honor of their son who had died three years before, and writers and scholars have benefited from substantial grant money every year since.

In 1922 at the University of Iowa in Iowa City, Carl Seashore, the Dean of Graduate Studies, set a precedent in higher education by allowing creative work to count as thesis for advanced degrees. That opened the door for Norman Foerster, the director of the School of Letters, to offer to select students writing classes that were taught by resident and visiting writers. In 1936, The Iowa Writers Workshop was born to then director Wilbur Schramm, and drew to its cradleside such luminaries as Robert Frost, Stephen Vincent Benet, John Berryman, Robert Penn Warren, and Robert Lowell. Since then, graduates have included Robert Bly, ZZ Packer, John Irving, W. P. Kinsella, Philip Levine, Nathan Englander, Mona Van Duyn, Bharati Mukherjee, Flannery O'Connor, Thom Jones, Thisbe Nissen, Jane Smiley, Rita Dove, and Michael Cunningham. The New School didn't get a graduate writing program until 1996, but back in 1931, Manhattan editor Gorham Munson started teaching his popular creative writing classes at what was then known as The New School for Social Research. In 1946, the Fulbright Scholarship was established, and the following year, Elliot Coleman started the prestigious Johns Hopkins program called The Writing Seminars.

■ BASIC TRAINING

A graduate writing program is housed at a university or college and has faculty that teach students of any adult age how to improve and hone their creative writing. There are required classes and workshops, writing of a book-length thesis, and sometimes the passing of a comprehensive exam. A writer applies to the graduate school, and if accepted, pays tuition and room and board to attend. In the end, a Master of Fine Arts or Master of Arts degree is conferred upon the student.

An artists colony or writers colony is usually located in a remote countryside near bodies of water, woods, or mountains and provides adult writers with the time, privacy, and space to work on their poetry, fiction, creative nonfiction, plays, or screenplays. There is a community of artists, writers, composers, dancers, and performing artists at many colonies, but sometimes there are only other writers. Evening meals offer opportunities to socialize, and respect is paid to anyone who wants to be left alone. A writer applies to a colony, and if accepted, usually pays only for travel expenses. There are no classes or required meetings, no chores, and at the end of your stay no one asks what you wrote or how much.

An artist-in-residency or writer-in-residency program is similar to a colony, except that only one person, not a group, is in residence at a National Park, historic home, community center, high school, college, or university at any given time. There is a requirement to give a talk or a reading, teach a class, and/or donate a piece of writing while in residence, but this should not take away from the time you spend on a specific writing project. A writer applies to this kind of program, and if accepted, must pay for travel, and buys and cooks their meals.

A grant or fellowship is an award of money—most often to enable a writer to spend more time writing. There are travel grants, special assistance grants, writing fellowships, and project grants. Some require you to report how the grant was used at the end of the year; others are simply awarded for work already written so as to encourage more of it. Certain state or regional fellowships are awarded with a stipulation that the recipient must do some community service for writers in the state or region. The recipient receives the money either all at once or in installments, and must pay tax on it the following year.

■ COMPARE AND CONTRAST

Suppose you have a quiet place to write that works for you most of the time but lately causes you to be distracted by this very quiet. Your close friends and colleagues are not writers, and you feel isolated by your lack of community. Whenever you open issues of *Poets & Writers* magazine or *The Writers Chronicle*, you see advertisements for MFA writing programs. Many of the contributors notes in the back of literary magazines list writers with MFA degrees from various colleges and universities. Maybe that is all you need to feel like a writer again. Should you apply for a graduate writing program?

The answer to this question depends on whether you feel isolated from a community or if you struggle with an isolation within your writing. If you are merely lonely for people who know what it feels like to write a book and deal with the waves of uncertainty and excitement, then you may benefit from attending an artists colony where you'll have a private studio and be able to dine and stroll with writers of different genres, artists of different disciplines, and composers of various kinds of music. It doesn't matter that you normally have a place to write that is tucked safely away from telephones and televisions, because that place has suddenly stopped your flow. If you are normally sure of yourself as a writer, and you might be writing a book that stems from an article or short story, then I advise getting the juices flowing again by staying for a month at an artists colony, or the more specific writers colony, where writers who are established and writers who are new enjoy each other's company and take inspiration from one another.

If, instead, you feel that you've come to a complete stop in your writing, turning in circles around the same subjects and approaches to the material, then attending a graduate writing program should help free you from that isolation in your work. A good graduate program is a mixture of reading, writing creatively, writing critically, exploring craft issues, learning to teach, and discovering a community of your peers. An MFA program in writing authorizes you through a student/mentor model, which is invigorating for writers who feel they are not getting attention for their work and want to explore new avenues.

Let's say that you are influenced by nature and are writing a collection of short stories on exotic birds and plant life. Should you apply for a travel grant? The answer to this question depends on whether you need to travel to specific locations to do research or the company of birds in their natural environment is inspiration enough. It may also matter how experienced you are in your craft, if you are well published, and if you also work in an ecological field. You can apply for travel grants, such as a Fulbright Scholarship or the Antarctic Writers & Artists Program; for writing fellowships that give you enough money to afford time off from work to travel, such as NEA or Guggenheim; for project grants, such as the Mary Roberts Rinehart Fund or the Money for Women/Barbara Deming Memorial Fund; or a two- or three-week residency in one of our national parks, such as the Everglades or Isle Royale National Park, where birds are aplenty.

Some will say that writing can't be taught, and I agree. Writing *can* be encouraged and improved, honed and perfected. The writer can become more adept at accessing his or her creative drive, a better self-editor and more confident. In fact, hypergraphia, the extreme desire to write, comes to us neurologically and is not easily dispelled.

How you become encouraged about your writing ability, how you improve, hone, or perfect it depends largely on your personality, and also on your professional engagement to the literary community to date. Every writer needs the time to write, a suitable environment, and money to support the writing life The right environment could be one that is guided by writing and literature professors and joined by other writers who want to explore new approaches in poetry, fiction, creative nonfiction, plays, and children's literature. The right environment could be a community center with a writing room that takes you away from home for a few days a week to work on a collection of poems without the usual distractions, and the other two days gives you a group of teenagers at that same center to inspire with poetry in performance classes after school. The right environment might be your own home, too, and a semester off from teaching at the local college because the state arts council grant came through and you'll still be able to pay rent without teaching.

Time is completely personal. You may be familiar with budgeting your time with your family and at work enough to consider getting your graduate writing degree at one of the evening programs, such as The New School, Northwestern, or Johns Hopkins, or at a low-residency program, such as Warren Wilson, Goddard, or Vermont College, which requires you spend twenty-five hours a week on your coursework, send homework to a faculty member every three weeks, and reside at the college for just ten days each semester. Or you may want to spread out your education and attend a graduate program that unfolds over three years, with interdisciplinary courses, writing workshops, and literature seminars during years one and two, and year three devoted to writing a book as thesis. Maybe you do not want anyone overseeing you while you write your libretto, graphic novel, or lyric essays because you already know what you want from the work and simply can't get it out of yourself if you're planning the family's schedules with no time to write. A room of your own—or for goodness' sake, a cottage of your own at MacDowell Colony or Hedgebrook for a month—will suit you perfectly. Or perhaps the freedom to travel would be most nourishing to your dormant imagination, and winning the Amy Lowell Poetry Travelling Scholarship for travel anywhere outside of North America for a year to write is just what the muses ordered.

And then there's the money. You'll be spending it to get an education, unless the program offers assistantships and fellowships, but an MFA degree will qualify you to teach at a college or university, for which you will be paid, and help you finish a book-length manuscript that will be of publishable quality. Academic writer-in-residence programs will pay you a stipend to be in residence, teach a few workshops, and give a public reading. But it is the grants and fellowships that enable you to pay bills, buy a new computer, travel for research, or take time off from your regular work commitments that are invaluable.

The reason you would get an MFA or MA degree in creative writing, apply to a colony or for a residency, or get a grant or fellowship is that one or all of these are opportunities for you to be a writer in the company of other writers, whether in the panel review process or in the classroom or on a ranch. The reason you would want to get an MFA or MA, apply for a colony or residency stay, or get a grant or fellowship is that to be a professional, published writer, you need to increase your visibility, and all of these are opportunities to be recognized.

In the next chapter, I'll help you with the applications, and in Chapters 3 through 5 I'll give you advice on how to choose from the many options out there.

2 Putting Your Best Foot Forward

Application Preparation Made Easy

■ GLOBAL POSITIONING

No matter at what stage—beginning, emerging, or established—you are in your writing career, you have goals. These will most likely be split between the work and the glory, as in "I want to write a novel" and "I want to be interviewed on *Charlie Rose* (NPR, *Today*, etc.)." We'll be focusing on the work goals (though the glory ones are important for every writer to nourish and visualize, too). Knowing what your goals are will help you determine the course you need to take to achieve them. Think of it as a kind of global positioning of your career in the larger literary society. Maybe you will apply for the American Antiquarian Association Creative and Performing Arts Writing Grant to do research on the Puritans for your historical novel, or apply to the Seattle Pacific University low residency MFA program to be trained among fellow writers who place their work within the larger context of Judeo-Christian faith.

You will need to define and express these goals on paper, placing yourself in relation to them—where you are, what you need. This is useful for two reasons. On the one hand, writing them down is like "magic imaging," the prehistoric man painting on the cave wall a picture of his spear arcing through the air and piercing the flank of the antelope before he goes out on the hunt and fells the live antelope to feed his family. On the other hand, writing your goals in a clear way is a requirement of the applications to graduate schools, colonies, residency programs, grants, and fellowships, and you can't get to them without it.

This part of an application is often called the artist statement or statement of intent, while other times these are separate statements and can each be one small paragraph or a small essay. Each program spells out its statement requirements: "Applicants must also submit a three- to four-page personal essay on their development as writers and a people of faith." (Seattle Pacific University); "send a one-page statement of intent that describes the potential of residency for professional growth, the specific focus of your project, relevancy of your writing and/or proposed project to the natural and cultural resources of Grand Canyon National Park." (AIR Program at Grand Canyon National Park); "a narrative Artists Statement (personal history, development as an artist, plans for the future) and a narrative Project Statement (project or activity to be undertaken, timeline, other sources of income for it)." (Cintas Fellowship).

Once you have identified the components that make up a typical statement, such as your development as a writer and plans for the future, you can begin to write a rough draft of an artist statement. However, if you are applying to different programs at the same time, you do not want to make the mistake of sending the same generic essay to every program on your list. The essay or statement might change slightly with regard to the opportunity you are seeking. For instance, you may apply to four different low-residency MFA programs, including Seattle Pacific University, but the others are not going to need to you to speak about the development of your faith and may want to know, instead, why their particular program would be helpful to you. You may be applying for a state arts grant and also a project grant, hoping that one or both will come through. A state arts council will ask for a statement no longer than one double-spaced page, whereas a project grant will require a budget, a plan for the use of the money, and a statement. In other words, one size does not fit all.

The New York Foundation for the Arts (NYFA) has posted on their website the artist statements of its recent fellowship winners, which include in 2005 nonfiction writers and poets. Reading through these is a great way to gauge the scope of the artist statement and the forms it takes, according to the particular writers and their goals. NYFA also includes the essays and excerpts of poetry that won. Below are three statements by Mark Bibbins, David Surface, and Melissa Haley, the writers who not only were among the winners of NYFA but were also nominated in 2005 for the NYFA Prize. NYFA fellowships are for $7,000, and $700 of that is withheld until the recipient satisfies the community service requirement. The NYFA Prize, which this year went to Melissa Haley, involves three separate selection committees and awards an additional $25,000.

According to the bio that accompanied the writing, artistic résumé, and artist statement of his application for a NYFA Fellowship, Mark Bibbins was born in Albany, New York, in 1968 and has lived in Manhattan since 1991. His first collection of poems, *Sky Lounge* (Graywolf Press, 2003), received a Lambda Literary Award. He teaches in the MFA program at The New School, where he was also a co-founder of *LIT* magazine. Individual poems of his have appeared in publications such as *Poetry*, *The Paris Review*, *The Yale Review*, *Boston Review*, and *Colorado Review*; others have been anthologized in *The Best American Poetry 2004*, *Great American Prose Poems*, *American Poetry: The Next Generation*, and elsewhere. He submitted the required ten pages of poetry, and this is his artist statement:

> I am sometimes wondering about the concept of a queer sensibility, and how such a thing (if there is one) makes its way from background to foreground (or if it should). Grammar, sex, salvation, travel, pollution, public television, and (especially) music have all been involved in the production of these poems. I should hope that they're capable of speaking for themselves now—in any event, they've stopped listening to me.

Bibbins gives us a kind of argument he has with himself about where his poetry comes from, the questionable queer influence on his identity as opposed to the actual ingredients of the poems. It amounts to his briefly describing the education of his poems, which are personified as autonomous, if not a bit rebellious, kids. The end humor, which rarely works in grant applications, is refreshing. Stylistically, Bibbins's use of parentheses to emphasize the argument of queer sensibility and the truth of his influences is poetic. And so, with this brief statement, we've been educated on Bibbins's artistic sensibility.

David Surface is a fiction writer, essayist, and journalist living in Brooklyn, New York. His stories and essays have been published in *DoubleTake*, *North American Review*, *Crazyhorse*, *Fiction*, and other literary magazines. He has been awarded residencies at the MacDowell Colony for the Arts and Dorland Mountain Arts Colony, and has twice been nominated for the Pushcart Prize in fiction. He is currently writer-in-residence at the Bronx High School for Writing and Communication Arts. He submitted the maximum requirement of twenty pages of nonfiction, along with this statement:

> When I write a story, I start with one true thing—a memory, an image, a sensation—then I try to say one more true thing, then another, and another. By the time I reach the end—hopefully—I've told the truth all the way through. It's harder than it sounds, harder than it ought to be. But still worth trying.

Surface's statement is instructive about what writing is like for him, where it originates, and how he pursues it, and also what the through-line is for him: truth. He's stated it quite simply and then negated the simplicity of it, while also, like the teacher he is, encouraged anyone reading it to persevere.

Melissa Haley is an archivist living in New York City. Her essays have appeared or are forthcoming in *The American Scholar*, *Commonplace*, and *Post Road*. She submitted the maximum requirement of twenty pages of nonfiction along with this statement:

> Whether I am writing essays or memoir, my work always tends toward two interrelated themes: a sense of history and a sense of place. As a historian and archivist, the stories I am drawn to are local ones, and I explore the ways in which setting and sensibility intertwine. Even when writing about my own life, I feel the need to bring the story outside of myself and, in some way, root it in history.

Haley reveals herself as a detective of history and presents the union of her interests in history and her home city. Her identity as a writer is intertwined with her occupation, and her writing is a way of locating herself in time. Her statement is all about where and who she is in her writing.

Although these are brief statements composed for fellowship applications, the precision of each and the writers' individual approaches to understanding the direction in their writing are instructive for anyone writing three-page essays to get into graduate school. You need to think about why you choose certain subjects for your work, why particular themes crop up, how you use language and imagery, and where you see yourself headed with the help of the MFA program to which you are applying.

■ THE WHEELS THAT TAKE YOU THERE

Another shared component for these opportunities is the sample of writing that you send with the application form. Always send the absolute best work you have. The graduate MFA and MA programs usually want a writing sample of twenty pages of prose or ten to fifteen pages of poetry, which makes it easy to choose work. Fiction and creative nonfiction writers should choose one whole story or essay over two or more excerpts, and poets should also keep from jumbling up a selection with wildly different styles and subjects. Some variation is welcome within the page limit, as long as you remember that complete strangers will be reading your writing to determine the strengths of your poetry; they won't have the benefit of context to inform their reading.

Artist-in-Residence (AIR) programs in the national parks ask for so few pages of writing (six to ten) as to both liberate and hobble the applicant, although poets have it easier. But since these programs often have an interest in supporting writers who would benefit from the natural history or cultural history of the park, you need send only writing that demonstrates an interest in these areas. Perhaps you plan to write a young adult novel about a boy who explores caves as a junior archaeologist and you would like a residency at Mammoth Cave National Park in Kentucky. If you have not started the book, you could send an excerpt of fiction that shows your faithful description of nature, animal life, or child adventurers. It is the combination of application materials that creates an impression, with emphasis placed on different parts. The national park AIR programs want only professional writers with a record of publishing, whereas Jentel Arts Colony and Ucross, on ranches down or up the road from each other in Wyoming, are interested in supporting writers at any stage of their careers who need uninterrupted weeks of peace and quiet to write.

■ RESUMING THE JOURNEY

The artistic résumé is a requirement of most grants and fellowships, artist-in-residency and writer-in-residency programs, and some colonies, although it is sometimes referred to as a CV, or curriculum vitae. The Guggenheim Foundation wants you to break out the parts of your résumé into complete sentences as "a brief narrative account of your career, describing accomplishments such as prizes, honors, or grants and fellowships (dates and grantors included)," which is separate from the detailed list of publications or productions you are also asked to include. If you don't have much to list on an artistic résumé and the inclusion of one is optional, don't worry; if it is mandatory, don't apply. Keep in mind that an artistic résumé should include publications, readings, awards and prizes won, and grants received. List the biggest and best first, such as books published, prizes won, and grants received. State arts councils often have guidelines for filling out the applications for their funding that include sample budgets for special assistance stipends (SOS) and sample résumés for literature fellowships; these samples can often be found on the councils' websites.

And while we're on the subject of applications, let me emphasize the importance of filling out application forms properly and including the exact number of copies of the materials required, exactly the type of materials required, presented exactly the way they want it. One exception to this rule are the state, regional, and city arts councils. The pool of applicants to these grants and fellowships are smaller than at nationwide foundation grants, and the administrators must support writers from their neck of the woods. If you are determined to be hasty in compiling application materials, your work may still be considered for state grants. But haste makes waste, literally, at the foundations and organizations offering open fellowships—an incorrectly completed application lands in the waste basket. Graduate writing programs and artist colonies have varying degrees of tolerance concerning improperly filled-out forms and excluded items, but why test them? Sure, it is annoying to make nine collated and stapled photocopies of a thirty-page double-spaced prose manuscript for the NEA, but that's the only way they'll consider you for a fellowship. And I'll add in that shrinking the typeface or narrowing the margins to get more words on the page is annoying to the panelists who read all the entries. Why annoy the people who have the power to choose your work? I have sat on panels and I can tell you that ten pages of poetry and twenty pages of prose is enough to know whether the writing is great or not so great. So choose your sample work wisely, and stay within the length limits.

One last suggestion: When you have decided the opportunities you want to pursue, start compiling the items that you'll need to photocopy and put them in a file in a drawer or on your computer, or both. This will save time, money, and space.

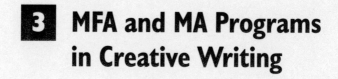 3 MFA and MA Programs in Creative Writing

There are two major elements to consider when determining which graduate writing program is right for you: the faculty and the program itself. Other considerations include location and cost, but these are contingent upon the first two. You really would not want to go to a writing program just because it is in a great locale; that said, terrific programs exist in inspiring locales. And as far as your budget goes, graduate students can get teaching assistantships at many MFA programs that remit their tuition and pay them a stipend.

■ FACULTY

Of course, you are going to gravitate to programs with your favorite writers attached, and that's a good start, but don't stop there. The faculty should be made up of professional writers who represent a broad spectrum of genres (unless it is a single-genre program) and aesthetics, who have published books, and who are approachable and knowledgeable. This will, inevitably, include a large number of writers with whom you will be unfamiliar. Part of the great experience of getting a master's degree in writing is exploring new ways of thinking about a specific genre through the perspectives of other practitioners in the field. Of course, with the advent of the low-residency graduate program, the faculty of which do not have to live and work where the university or college is located, any one writer may be a faculty member at two writing programs and, when a new book is out and well-reviewed, a visiting writer at many more. I'm even aware of a writer who directs one MFA program and teaches at another. This may not bode well for those MFA graduates who hope to make a living by teaching, but it relates to another important criteria for choosing a writing program by its faculty: The writers who teach you should be working writers if you are to gain insight and experience on building a career for yourself. A mix of full-time faculty and visiting writers will give you the opportunity to study with different professors each semester, but when you are perusing the faculty lists, you should keep in mind that a few universities, such as Houston, Columbia, and NYU, have famous-name writers teaching only one semester a year.

■ PROGRAM

In the last ten years, the graduate writing program has evolved like Darwin's finches, and I suggest you peruse the list I've compiled with an open, eager mind. I promise you will begin to imagine aspects of an MFA in creative writing that you never would have guessed—a Peace Corps stint, collaborations with video artists, conversations with

Ezra Pound's family at an alpine castle, and more—and refine your wish list accordingly.

You can attend a graduate school full-time or part-time, while residing at the college for two or three solid years or a month total over the course of two years, and you can study one genre, or two or more, and combine with other art forms. Graduate programs are becoming increasingly international, offering students opportunities to think globally, read literature across national and cultural borders, learn from international authors, and become fluent enough to translate other writings into English. Social justice, faith, art, and ethics play parts in defining new programs.

Traditionally, a graduate creative writing program lasted two years and was taught in two separate genres only, poetry and fiction. These writers enrolled in the college or university lived on- or off-campus until graduation. They were either awarded a Master of Fine Arts or a Master of Arts degree in creative writing. About thirty years ago, the poet Ellen Bryant Voigt devised a largely correspondence-based MFA program for writers who headed families and held down jobs that prevented them from pursuing graduate school in other parts of the country. Her low-residency model of study, which took the form of a tutorial during each semester and included a ten-day residency at the college with writing workshops, craft classes, readings, and events, has been replicated and revised over the years. When creative nonfiction became a hot new genre, Goucher College created its low-residency single-genre program for writers of creative nonfiction, which they define the most broadly of all—personal essay, memoir, narrative nonfiction, literary journalism, travel/nature/science writing, biography, and professional writing. Although many programs were hesitant to think of any nonfiction as creative writing, they are now attracting more students by offering it as a possible concentration of study. Of course, creative nonfiction has helped to welcome the idea of mixed-genre writing and multigenre writers, and art schools have welcomed these distinctions in their new expansive MFA programs in creative writing. The new kids on the block are playwrights and children's book writers.

The Associated Writers and Writing Programs (AWP) states that the MFA is a terminal degree, by which they mean that those who hold that degree have enough accreditation to teach writing at the college level. No need for a Ph.D. or a post-MFA certificate. You should note that they also believe that the art of writing is qualification enough aside from an MFA degree, and that authors of novels, poetry, short stories, essays, and memoirs are good candidates for teaching. You have to have a BA to go for an MFA, in most cases, although you do not always need to have taken the GRE.

A good graduate creative writing program, whether MFA or MA, will have a strong curriculum. Some writing programs balance the work between writing workshops and literature courses, with electives on craft issues and other academic subjects pertinent to the students' work. Other programs offer very little diversion from the development of writing. Most programs do not spend much, if any, time on educating students about the publishing world or what alternatives to teaching are available to them when they graduate. Those that do take it upon themselves to educate writers about their careers invite editors and agents to meet with students, bring in successful alumni to talk about career paths, pay for graduate assistantships on literary journals and university presses, and even offer courses in publishing and internships with arts organizations.

You may choose to go to school just to have more time to write and explore new voices. Brown University requires of its students only eight courses in two years, half in writing and half in electives.

About a quarter of the graduate programs are three or more years long, although some of those pile on more credits with each additional year. The writing of a book-length creative thesis, or manuscript, is the goal of every program, and some programs, such as at the University of Minnesota, reserve the entire third year, instead of a single semester, to the creation of this publishable book.

You can get an MFA degree in beautiful places, such as Alaska, Montana, Florida, New Mexico, Arizona, or California, and you can attend on full scholarships and teaching assistantships with stipends. You can join a workshop online, write a critical paper in your own backyard, and spend parts or all of a semester in another country. The choice is yours, and the opportunities get better every year as the program directors keep apace of the literary and real world.

The CD-ROM included in this book contains all the listings below and more—forty MA and 114 MFA programs in all. I selected the sixty programs described below based on several criteria: 1. fame or prestige; 2. modern approach; 3. flexibility; 4. writing life; 5. cost.

Fame or prestige is self-explanatory. Modern approach includes multi-genres, mixed genres, socially conscious programs, global issues, and collaborations. Flexibility includes degrees of three or more years, part-time, distance-learning, and low-residency programs. The writing life includes those that instruct students to teach at secondary and college levels, in traditional and nontraditional settings, offer experience in editing and publishing, or arts administration, opportunities to meet editors and agents, and learn the basics of publishing and building a career. Cost refers to any financial aid, whether federal loans, graduate or teaching assistantships, fellowships, or scholarships that defray the cost of going to school in writing. The entries are listed alphabetically rather than ranked, and descriptions are certainly not all-inclusive. Not all programs offer perks or ways to defray costs. The part-time and low residency programs do not offer graduate or teaching assistantships because students do not reside full-time. The part-time aspect allows the students to make livings at jobs instead, which funds their education. Perks such as editorial experience with literary journals and university presses are also dependent on a full-time faculty and student base, which is missing in a low residency program. This is a list to whet your appetite, and I encourage you to follow the links on the CD to all the other colleges and universities that offer students the chance to find their voices in poetry, fiction, creative nonfiction, plays, screenplays, hypertext, hybrid forms, children's literature, and whatever else we may come up with in the meantime.

Sixty MFA and MA Creative Writing Degree Programs

University of Alabama, Tuscaloosa
www.bama.ua.edu/~writing

DEGREE: a three- to four-year, 48 credit residency program for writers of poetry, fiction, nonfiction, film writing, or digital media, resulting in a book-length thesis, orally defended, and a Master of Fine Arts degree in creative writing

PERKS: Writers-in-residence, *Black Warrior Review*, Bankhead Visiting Writers Series

NUTSHELL: The Program in Creative Writing at the University of Alabama, in the river city of Tuscaloosa—which comes from a Choctaw word for "Black Warrior"—is one of the most respected in this country. It has adapted itself over the years to accommodate the changing passions of both its faculty and students so that the genres of digital media, film writing, and nonfiction could be offered in conjunction with the study of poetry and fiction, which is also reflected in the school's literary journal, *Black Warrior Review*, and its culturally diverse Bankhead Visiting Writers Series. The studio/academic program requires writing workshops, forms courses, and literature classes with topics such as "The Alphabet from Sand to Silicon," "The Visual Book," "Modes of Political Poetry," "Teaching Creative Writing," and "Poetry & Dance." Students are allowed to submit theses, which are not print-based.

FACULTY: Robin Behn, Joel Brouwer, Sandra Huss, Joyelle McSweeney, Michael Martone, Wendy Rawlings, and Patti White

DEFRAYING THE COST: The graduate program at Tuscaloosa is committed to providing financial support to all students for as long as four years. Incoming students get Graduate Teaching Assistantships, enabling them to teach "Freshman Composition" and "Introduction to Literature" classes, for $10,007 stipends over nine months and full tuition remission, or are eligible for Graduate Council Fellowships of $14,000 and full tuition remission without teaching requirements. For their students' second years (and beyond) the stipends for teaching assistantships increase to $10,407 along with tuition remission, and give recipients the chances to teach "Introduction to Creative Writing," "Poetry Writing" and "Fiction Writing."

Sandy Huss, The Program in Creative Writing, University of Alabama, Department of English, P.O. Box 870244, Tuscaloosa, AL 35487-0244, 205-348-0766, shuss@english.as.ua.edu

---

"In my experience, CalArts MFA Writing program's greatest strength is its ability to welcome and facilitate experimental and cross-genre/interdisciplinary writing. As a graduate student there, it was a great pleasure to take Visual Arts critical theory courses and to have the opportunity to interact with MFA students pursuing a wide range of conceptual and creative endeavors beyond writing."

—Felicia Luna Lemus, author of *Trace Elements of Random Tea Parties* (Farrar, Straus & Giroux, 2003)

University of Alaska–Anchorage
http://cwla.uaa.alaska.edu

DEGREE: a two-and-a-half-year, 45 credit resident program for writers of fiction, poetry, and creative nonfiction, resulting in a book-length thesis, in-depth critical essay, and Master of Fine Arts degree in creative writing

PERKS: *Understory, Alaska Quarterly Review*, LitSite Alaska; student readings, visiting writers, The Writing Rendezvous, Chugach Mountains

NUTSHELL: A flexible, professional program designed to accommodate each student's needs, the Department of Creative & Literary Arts prepares students for various careers—including those involving professional writing, teaching, and editing—with research assistant-ships and teaching assistantships. The University produces an under-graduate magazine, *Understory*, the acclaimed national literary journal *The Alaska Quarterly Review*, and the online community LitSite Alaska, and hosts The Writing Rendezvous festival. The emphasis of courses is balanced between the study and practice of craft and the study of form and theory as they relate to style and content. Work-shops are interactive courses where students produce original works of literature and engage in productive critiques of each other's writing. The classes and writing culminate in a book-length work of fiction, po-etry, drama, or creative nonfiction and a thesis defense, including an in-depth craft essay that puts the student's book into critical perspective.

FACULTY: Linda McCarriston, Jo-Ann Mapson, Sherry Simpson, and Ronald Spatz

DEFRAYING THE COST: There are various award packages available, in-cluding a full tuition waiver for up to nine graduate credits, which is $4,482 per semester for nonresidents, or $8,964 per year. Students can apply to be research assistants on *The Alaska Quarterly Review*, *Understory*, or LitSite Alaska, or apply to be teaching assistants within the College of Arts and Sciences for $2,500 a semester, or $5,000 a year. The assistantship positions require a ten-hour a week commitment from recipients. Financial aid and loan counseling are also available.

Sabrina M. Haverfield, Administrative Assistant, Department of Creative Writing & Literary Arts, The University of Alaska–Anchorage, AK 99508, 907-786-4330, ycwla@uaa.alaska.edu

University of Alaska–Fairbanks
www.uaf.edu/english

DEGREE: a three-year, 45 credit resident program for writers of poetry, fiction, nonfiction, and plays, culminating in a book-length thesis, orally defended, and a Master of Fine Arts degree in creative writing

PERKS: *Permafrost, ICEBOX,* writers-in-residence, Alaskan wilderness, aurora borealis, Fairbanks Symphony Orchestra

NUTSHELL: One of fifty-one Master's degree programs at Fairbanks, the MFA in creative writing has been going strong since 1968, with small workshops fostering close relationships between members of the faculty and students. Besides the 360 million acres of wilderness, dogsledding, fishing, and skiing, and the aurora borealis streaking across the night sky, Fairbanks offers its graduate students teaching opportunities and editing experience with the literary journal *Permafrost,* and hosts reading series. The curriculum includes writing workshops, craft classes, and modern and contemporary literature courses. Students also benefit from the influence of writers-in-residence, such as Hilda Raz, Mary Gaitskill, Toi Derricotte, Paula Gunn Allen, Lewis Nordan, and Alice Fulton.

FACULTY: Anne Caston, Renee Manfredi, John Reinhard, and Frank Soos

DEFRAYING THE COST: Fifteen teaching assistantships are available at a beginning stipend of $8,740, with tuition waiver and yearly increases.

Department of English, University of Alaska–Fairbanks, Fairbanks, AK 99775-5720, 907-474-7193, faengl@uaf.edu

American University
www.american.edu/cas/lit/mfa-lit.htm

DEGREE: a two- to four-year full-time resident or part-time program for writers of poetry, fiction, plays, and screenplays, culminating in a book-length thesis and a Master of Fine Arts degree in creative writing

PERKS: visiting writers series, writers-in-residence, *Folio*, *In Capital Letters*, *The Messenger*, Lannan Poetry Program

NUTSHELL: Established in 1980 and aligned with the masters program in literature, the Masters of Fine Arts in creative writing challenges students in the craft of writing and offers them a safe place to take creative risks. Students are also free to explore more than one genre. The program fosters a noncompetitive environment and an open, supportive community while opening students up to the rich literary community of Washington, D.C. and the ways they might support themselves within it. Internships with the Visiting Writers Series, the twice-yearly *Folio: A Literary Journal*, or the newsletters *In Capital Letters* and *The Messenger*, and teaching assistantships with the Writing Center or with professors of English round out the experience of writing workshops, literature seminars, and classes on journalism and translation. Graduates include Maxine Clair, Carolyn Parkhurst, Leslie Pietrzyk, and Liz Poliner.

FACULTY: Kyle Dargan, Andrew Holleran, E. J. Levy, Richard McCann, Kermit Moyer, Denise Orenstein, David Rowell, Myra Sklarew, and Henry Taylor

DEFRAYING THE COST: Besides financial aid, the university gives merit awards to students who work up to twenty hours a week, at hourly compensation, in the writing center or as teaching assistants to professors of general education or undergraduate literature courses. Occasionally, there are work-study assistantships for up to ten hours a week in the writing center.

Kermit Moyer, Richard McCann, Myra Sklarew, Henry Taylor, Codirectors, MFA Program in Creative Writing, American University, Department of Literature, 4400 Massachusetts Avenue NW, Washington, D.C. 20016, 202-885-2990, kwmoyer@american.edu

Antioch University, Los Angeles
www.antiochla.edu/MFA

DEGREE: a two- to two-and-a-half-year, 48-60 credit low-residency program for writers of poetry, fiction, and creative nonfiction, resulting in a book-length manuscript, public reading, lecture, and a Master of Fine Arts degree in creative writing

PERKS: the temperate and scenic Marina del Rey in June and December

NUTSHELL: Antioch emphasizes the social and ethical issues related to the role of the writer in contemporary society and pluralistic culture, and expects diverse perspectives of aesthetics and voice. Single-genre concentrations take two years and 48 credits, and dual-genre concentrations require an additional semester and total of 60 credits. Each semester starts with a ten-day residency in Marina del Rey and continues at home with correspondence with a faculty mentor. In the fourth semester, each student teaches a senior seminar and presents a reading from his or her book-length manuscript. During the residencies, courses in potential career paths for writers are available.

FACULTY: Chris Abani, Dodie Bellamy, Brian Bouldrey, Susan Taylor Chehak, Hope Edelman, Richard Garcia, Frank Gaspar, Eloise Klein Healy, Steve Heller, Dana Johnson, Brad Kessler, Jim Krusoe, Peter Levitt, Brenda Miller, Carol Potter, Sharman Russell, David Starkey, Lisa Teasley, David Ulin, Alma Luz Villanueva, and Nancy Zafris

DEFRAYING THE COST: The cost of attending the low-residency MFA program in creative writing ranges from $4,960 to $7,965 per semester. Up to $800 per student is available through Antioch Opportunity Grants and Eloise Klein Healy Grants. Financial aid is also available.

MFA in Creative Writing Program, 400 Corporate Pointe, Culver City, CA 90230, 310-578-1090 or 800-7-ANTIOCH, admissions@antiochla.edu

Arizona State University
www.asu.edu

DEGREE: a two-year, 48-60 credit interdisciplinary program for writers of poetry, fiction, creative nonfiction, plays, and screenplays, resulting in a book-length manuscript, reading, and a Master of Fine Arts degree in creative writing

PERKS: *Hayden's Ferry Review*; Community Writers' Workshop; visiting editors, writers, and artists; high-school outreach program

NUTSHELL: A modern, interdisciplinary program run jointly by the Department of English and the College of Liberal Arts and Sciences and the Department of Theatre in the College of Fine Arts that encourages collaborative production with musicians, fine printers, and visual artists. It gives equal weight to literature and writing, and requires of its graduates a final comprehensive exam that covers twentieth-century literature and critical theory for writers of poetry and prose, and European and American drama and dramatic theory and criticism for playwrights. Students can get experience in editing and production while working with the nationally recognized literary journal *Hayden's Ferry Review*, directing a conference with the ASU Community Writers' Workshop, or teaching by mentoring kids as part of the high-school outreach program. The visiting writers, editors, and artists series focus on issues of building a career and publishing. Graduates include Mary Gannon and Rick Noguchi.

FACULTY: Jay Boyer, Ron Carlson, Norman Dubie, Beckian Fritz Goldberg, Cynthia Hogue, T. M. McNally, Paul Morris, Melissa Pritchard, Guillermo Reyes, Jewell Parker Rhodes, Alberto Rios, and Jeannine Savard

DEFRAYING THE COST: Virginia G. Piper Writing Center Fellowships include the $25,000 Theresa A. Wilhoit MFA Thesis Fellowship for third-year MFA students and the $5,000 Virginia G. Piper Summer Fellowships for first- and second-year students to do research or creative activity.

Karla Elling, Program Coordinator, Creative Writing Program, Arizona State University, Department of English, Tempe, AZ 85287-0302,

480-965-9011 (tel.), 480-965-3451 (fax), information@asu.edu or karla.elling@asu.edu

University of Arizona
http://w3.arizona.edu/~cwp

DEGREE: a two-year, 36 credit program for writers of poetry, fiction, and creative nonfiction, resulting in a book-length creative thesis and a Master of Fine Arts degree with a major in creative writing

PERKS: *Suntracks*, visiting writers, ArtsReach, *Sonora Review*, Tucson, Kore Press, *Arizona Quarterly*, *Saguaro*, *Persona*, Poetry Center

NUTSHELL: Twenty-five years old, Arizona's MFA program encourages students to shape their own study within the context of the required four workshops, two seminars, and six electives to reach a publishable manuscript. Students take one creative writing craft seminar in the chosen genre and in another one—such as "Nonfiction of the Southwest" or "Poetry of the 90s"—and writing workshops with four different members of the faculty. The electives can be in any of the university's departments—such as Film and Anthropology—not just English and Literature. Arizona awards teaching assistantships for two sections of freshman composition, and sometimes one section of introductory creative writing classes. Further work experience is gained by editing the *Sonora Review*, Kore Press, *Sun-Tracks*, *Arizona Quarterly*, *Saguaro*, and *Persona*. The University of Arizona Poetry Center grant brings a poet-in-residence to the school during the summer.

FACULTY: Jon Anderson, Jason Brown, Alison Hawthorne Deming, Elizabeth Evans, Robert Houston, Jane Miller, Steve Orlen, C. E. Poverman, Boyer Rickel, Aurelie Sheehan, Richard Shelton, and Peter Wild

DEFRAYING THE COST: Arizona awards about a dozen teaching assistantships a year that are based on an evaluation of students' creative samples by the faculty admissions committees in each genre. This translates to a waiver of nonresident tuition in addition to an annual salary ranging from $11,939 (for those with a BA) to $12,735 (for those who also have an MA). Students pay for registration fees. Out-of-state tuition waivers and prizes and awards are also available.

Robert Houston, Director of Creative Writing, University of Arizona, Department of English, Tucson, AZ 85721-0067, 520-621-3880 (tel.), cwp@3.arizona.edu

The School of the Art Institute of Chicago
www.artic.edu

DEGREE: a two-year, 60 credit resident program for writers of poetry, fiction, creative nonfiction, essays, scripts, and image/text, culminating in a book-length thesis and a Master of Fine Arts degree in creative writing

PERKS: visiting artists and writers, collaborations with artists and musicians

NUTSHELL: A flexibly structured program conceived by the faculty of writers, performers, film and video makers, visual communicators, printmakers, and painters as a way to encourage hybrid works, new forms, and collaborative projects. To this end, students may choose each semester's faculty adviser from the core writing faculty or the schoolwide graduate roster of professors in all the arts, and can supplement their graduate project of advisory sessions and writing workshops with electives in art history, arts administration, theory and criticism, liberal arts, and historic preservation. Further opportunities await students in art-related internships in the Chicago area and other U.S. cities, and in lectures and critiques by visiting artists, writers, and scholars.

FACULTY: Carol Anshaw, Dan Beachy-Quick, Carol Becker, Rosellen Brown, Elizabeth Cross, Mary Cross, Janet Desaulniers, Amy England, Calvin Forbes, Matthew Goulish, Sara Levine, James McManus, Michael K. Meyers, Beth Nugent, Peter O'Leary, Elise Paschen, Jill Riddell, David Robbins, George H. Roeder Jr., Ellen Rothenberg, and Mary Margaret Sloane

DEFRAYING THE COST: The program offers extensive financial aid, as well as teaching assistantships in undergraduate classes and graduate assistantships in office programs.

MFA in Writing Degree Program, The School of the Art Institute of Chicago, Chicago, IL 60603-6110, 800-232-7242 (T), 312-899-1840 (F), admiss@artic.edu

Boise State University
www.boisestate.edu/english/mfa

DEGREE: a two-year, 48-credit resident program for writers of poetry and fiction, resulting in a book-length creative thesis and Master of Fine Arts degree in creative writing

PERKS: *Ahsahta Press, Idaho Review*, writer-in-residence program

NUTSHELL: Diverse faculty encourage students to focus on their craft, but provide plenty of opportunities to develop skills in magazine editing and managing with the *Idaho Review* and book production and promotion with Ahsahta Press and the Sawtooth Prize. In the spring, a writer-in-residence teaches a graduate course and gives public readings. These residents have included Alvin Greenberg and Stephanie Strickland. Additionally, the program invites writers such as Rae Armantrout, Rick Bass, Charles Baxter, Claudia Keelan, and Alice Notley to give readings.

FACULTY: Janet Holmes, Elise Blackwell, and Mitchell Weiland

DEFRAYING THE COST: Teaching assistantships are competitive but grant full tuition waivers and annual stipends.

Janet Holmes, English Department, Boise State University, 1910 University Drive, Boise, ID 83725-1525, 208-426-2669, www.boisestate.edu

Bowling Green State University
www.bgsu.net

DEGREE: a two-year, 40-credit resident program for writers of poetry and fiction, resulting in a book-length creative thesis, an oral examination, and a Master of Fine Arts degree in creative writing

PERKS: Arts & Sciences Distinguished Visiting Writer

NUTSHELL: One of the most well-known and respected creative writing programs that provides developing fiction writers or poets with training in the techniques of their genre, continuous practice in writing, and detailed criticisms of their work. The program allows students to choose electives such as desktop publishing and creative writing program administration for a leg up on the job search, or in the academic departments of philosophy, physics, history, and art. The correlation between the electives and writing does not have to be great, as long as the students explore possibilities and develop their own writing style as fully as possible under the direction of competent and experienced instructors.

FACULTY: Sharona Ben-Tov, Lawrence Coates, Michael Czyzniejewski, Wendell Mayo, Larissa Szporluk, and John Wylum

DEFRAYING THE COST: All qualified students who want Teaching Assistantships receive them, which is usually everyone. There are also The Devine Memorial Fellowships awarded to four students each summer.

Lawrence Coates, Director, Creative Writing, Bowling Green State University, Bowling Green, OH 43403, 419-372-2531,
mcGowa@bgnet.bgsu.edu

University of British Columbia
www.creativewriting.ubc.ca

DEGREE: a three- to five-year, 36-credit low-residency program for writers of poetry, fiction, nonfiction, children's books, translation, plays, and screenplays, resulting in a book-length creative thesis and a Master of Fine Arts degree in creative writing

PERKS: Vancouver; multigenre, online workshops

NUTSHELL: This first Canadian low-residency program allows students who can't make a two-year commitment to Vancouver to indulge in the seven-genre studio program for multigenre exploration. UBC focuses on creative writing instead of critical writing, and immerses students in three genres (fiction, nonfiction, and poetry) during the first year, and the remainder of the genres (screenwriting, playwriting, writing for children, and translation) during the second and third years. Students are required to work in at least three genres during the course of their years in the program. Truly flexible, UBC lets students take as few as one class during a semester, as long as the degree is completed in five years. Unlike the originating tutorial model of the low-residency MFA, UBC restores the multi-critique approach in online workshops during the semesters away. What's more, this is really an "optional-residency" program, since students can opt-out of the *one* residency a year, in July, and attend entirely electronically. Courses include "Constructing Literature from the Found Materials of the Known World" and "The Past That Breaks Out in Our Hearts."

FACULTY: Gail Anderson-Dargatz, Zsuzs Gartner, Gary Geddes, Terry Glavin, and Susan Musgrave

DEFRAYING THE COST: It costs $766.66 Canadian per credit for U.S. and International students and $466.66 per credit for Canadian students. It comes to $27,600 Canadian over three to five years. Usually,

Americans make out better in the exchange rate, but you'll have to figure it out when the time comes. The only way to defray this overall cost is to apply for financial aid.

Creative Writing Program of the Department of Theatre, Film and Creative Writing, University of British Columbia, Buch. E462-1866 Main Mall, Vancouver, British Columbia V6T 1Z1, Canada, 604-822-0699, Patrose@uning.ubc.edu

Brown University
www.brown.edu/Departments/English/Writing

DEGREE: a two-year resident program for writers of poetry, fiction, hypertext, and plays, resulting in a manuscript and a Master of Fine Arts degree in literary arts

PERKS: visiting writers, Chinese dissident writers, Burning Deck Press, Paradigm Press, Lost Roads Publishing

NUTSHELL: This program was begun in the 1960s by poet and critic Edwin Honig as a creative writing MFA, but underwent a name change in 2003. It is an avant-garde haven, granting its students maximum time to write and explore hypertext and mixed-media forms, as well as experimental fiction, poetry, and plays. Students need take only *eight* courses over the entire two years, half in writing and half in electives. Students may select their electives from any of Brown's course offerings, including studio art, translation, literature, history, philosophy, theater arts, modern culture and media, religious studies, and foreign languages. The final semester is reserved for the thesis.

There's a great literary community on campus with readings, festivals, and performances that expose students to the contemporary scene. This is a socially conscious program, inviting international writers who feel they cannot use free expression at home to reside for a year at Brown.

FACULTY: Ama Ata Aidoo, Robert Coover, Brian Evanson, Thalia Field, Forrest Gander, Michael S. Harper, George Lamming, Carole Maso, Gail Nelson, Aishah Rahman, Meredith Steinbach, Paula Vogel, Keith Waldrop, John Edgar Wideman, Erin Cressida Wilson, and C. D. Wright

DEFRAYING THE COST: Brown offers fellowships, scholarships, teaching assistantships, and proctorships to those who apply for financial aid. The graduate program seeks to grant financial aid to every student in their program, usually fifteen a year, and in the last decade they have succeeded. Typically, a first-year student receives a fellowship or proctorship that pays a small monthly stipend and covers tuition, the health fee, and health insurance. Proctorships are for nonacademic employment for a limited number of hours per week, while fellowships are awarded in recognition of merit and personal need, and do not require employment. A second-year qualified student in good standing will be awarded a teaching assistantship to teach one undergraduate writing workshop per semester, and receive in payment a full stipend, tuition, health fee, and health insurance.

Forrest Gander, Director, Graduate Program in Literary Arts, Brown University, Box 1852, Providence, RI 02912, 401-863-3260, Writing@brown.edu

California College of the Arts
www.cca.edu

DEGREE: a two-year, 60-credit resident program for writers of poetry, short fiction, novels, creative nonfiction, and scripts, resulting in a book-length manuscript in one specific discipline or a combination, and a Master of Fine Arts degree in writing

PERKS: *Eleven Eleven*; visiting writers, art and design classes

NUTSHELL: A program developed by writers for writers at an independent art and design school so that writers can experiment with image and text, performance art, book art, video and film art, media arts, and cyber arts, as well as the basic genres of short story, novel, poetry, creative nonfiction, and scripts. Through traditional and innovative practice, personal exploration and collaboration are sought. The goal is to turn out writers who can work in a variety of milieus and forms and who feel comfortable in a community of artists. Reading-intensive elective seminars, writing workshops, and one-on-one mentoring define this program with course offerings as seemingly simple as workshops in poetry, fiction, and creative nonfiction, and as adventurous as the interdisciplinary course called "The Complete Fresco" and the literature course titled "My Mother Is a Fish!"

FACULTY: Juvenal Acosta, Opal Palmer Adisa, Stephen Ajay, Tom Barbash, Rick Barot, Hugh Behm-Steinberg, Rebekah Bloyd, Sydney Carson, Betsy Davids, Doug Dorst, Kathleen Fraser, Gloria Frym, Eliza Harding, John Laskey, Joseph Lease, Denise Newman, Michelle Richmond, Jack Rogow, Judith Serin, Ann Joslin Williams, and Cooley Windsor

DEFRAYING THE COST: It costs $27,110 per year to attend CCA, a school that prides itself on being accessible and affordable. Each year, renewable CCA Graduate Merit Scholarships of $7,000 to $12,500 are granted to outstanding students; renewable diversity scholarships for $4000 to $12,500 to students who bring diverse experiences, ideas, and creative work to the community; graduate need-based scholarships of $1,000 to $9,000; graduate teaching assistantships for $2,000 per semester; and federal and state grants, student loans, and work-study programs.

Ann Joslin Williams, Chair, MFA Program in Writing, California College of the Arts, 1111 Eighth St., San Francisco, CA 94107-2247, 415-703-9500, graduateprograms@cca.edu

---

"At NYU, I never felt any pressure to conform to a particular mode of writing. More important, the school's outreach programs are well-established—as a *New York Times* Fellow, I taught writing at a public high school, one of many opportunities to interact with the community. Also, you can pursue either an MFA or an MA with a concentration in creative writing, a valuable option for those who want the flexibility of a literature degree. The alumni presence is strong and generous—former classmates often solicit story submissions and give leads on jobs and agents."

—Dika Lam, winner of The Bronx Writers Center 2005 Chapter One contest.

California Institute of the Arts
www.calarts.edu/~writing

DEGREE: a two-year, 36-credit resident program for writers of fiction, nonfiction, poetry, screenplays, mixed media, and hybrid forms, resulting in a book-length creative thesis and a Master of Fine Arts degree in creative writing

PERKS: writer-in-residence, visiting writers, *Trepan*, *Black Clock*

NUTSHELL: Located within the School of Critical Studies at an art school dedicated to experimental practice, this program teaches students to question the distinctions between critical and creative writing, theoretical and practical writing, and experimental and conventional approaches. Students can branch out or double up in their pursuit of artistic expression by applying for the Integrated Media Program or another MFA program in art, dance, music, film/video, or theater at the same time as the writing program. CalArts has a diverse faculty, visiting writer series, and writer-in-residence program to encourage critical writers to think about form, aesthetics, rhetoric, and mode of presentation and creative writers to consider critical ideas for the structure and drive in their work. CalArts produces two literary journals: *Trepan*, entirely edited by graduate students, and *Black Clock*, edited by Steve Erickson. Workshops and seminars range from analytical essays to new fiction, and specific discussions of how pornography has influenced contemporary culture or how one hundred fifty people collaborated on one book keep students aware of their changing world.

FACULTY: Bernard Cooper, John D'Agata, Steve Erickson, Peter Gadol, David St. John, Janet Sarbanes, Mady Schutzman, Matias Viegener, John Wagner, and Christine Wertheim

DEFRAYING THE COST: CalArts offers teaching assistantships, editorial assistantships, and technology assistantships.

Dwayne Moser, MFA Program Coordinator, California Institute of the Arts, 24700 McBean Pkwy., Valencia, CA 91355, 661-253-7701, Dmoser@calarts.edu

University of California–Irvine
www.humanities.uci.edu/english

DEGREE: a two-year, 72-credit resident program for writers of poetry and fiction, resulting in a book-length creative thesis and a Master of Fine Arts degree in English

PERKS: visiting writers and lecturers, MFA Reading Series, Digital Library

NUTSHELL: This small program, started in 1965, centers on the Graduate Writing Workshop, in which faculty and students share in criticism and discussion of student writing. The one requirement is for students of this program to one day write something that lasts, and to help them reach this goal, Irvine keeps the student body small—ten to twelve in each genre—and chooses applicants who wish to make writing their life. Graduates include Aimee Bender, Michael Chabon, Jill Ciment, Richard Ford, and Frank X. Gaspar.

FACULTY: Oakley Hall, Michelle Latiolais, James McMichael, Michael Ryan, and Geoffrey Wolff

DEFRAYING THE COST: The Department of English and Comparative Literature supports the graduate students with teaching assistantships. Out-of-state tuition waivers are also available.

Administrator, The MFA Programs in Writing, Department of English and Comparative Literature, University of California–Irvine, Irvine, CA 92697-2650, 949-824-6718, aread@uci.edu

Carlow University
www.carlow.edu

DEGREE: a flexible, 36-credit low-residency program for writers of poetry, fiction, and creative nonfiction, resulting in a publishable full-length manuscript and a Master of Fine Arts degree in creative writing

PERKS: visiting writers, Ireland, Pittsburgh, Marilyn P. Donnelly Writers Series, Focus on Women lecture series, International Poetry Forum

NUTSHELL: A practical program that focuses on writing as a vocation for adult writers, primarily women, who want to do intensive work in writing and make a rigorous study of literature but do not wish to learn how to teach at colleges and universities. The coursework is individually designed for the student with the help of the American and Irish faculty, who have only five students at a time and who communicate during the five semesters consistently via e-mail and the Internet—specifically, through Carlow's convenient Blackboard system of message and information posting. The eleven-day residencies are at Carlow University in Pittsburgh, Pennsylvania, in January, and St. Patrick's–Carlow College in Carlow, Ireland, in June. The Marilyn P. Donnelly Distinguished Writers-in-Residence Series has brought Louise Gluck, Desmond Egan, and Naomi Shihab Nye to the campuses, and the Focus on Women series of lectures has presented such authors as Margaret Atwood, Nikki Giovanni, and Germaine Greer.

Students benefit from access to the renowned International Poetry Forum archives, housed at the college, and the rich literary life of Pittsburgh.

FACULTY: Vivienne Abbott, David Baker, Jan Beatty, Pat Boren, David Butler, Jane Candia Coleman, Ita Daly, Gerald Dawe, Patricia Dobler, Desmond Egan, Janice Eidus, Anne Enright, Robert Gibb, Vona Groarke, Sean Hardie, Eugene McCabe, Dinty Moore, Conor O'Callaghan, Mary O'Donnell, Ann Townsend, Marion Winik, and Ellie Wymard

DEFRAYING THE COST: Financial aid is available, as are Corporate Scholarships for those employed by corporations affiliated with Carlow University. The scholarships reduce the cost per credit by 25 percent.

Graduate Admissions, Carlow College, 3333 Fifth Ave., Pittsburgh, PA 15213-3109, 800-333-CARLOW, www.gradstudies.carlow.edu/mfa_writing.html

Columbia College—Fiction
www.fiction.colum.edu

DEGREES: a two-and-a-half-year, 45-credit resident program for writers of fiction, creative nonfiction, and plays, resulting in a book-length creative thesis and a Master of Fine Arts degree in creative writing; or a 39-credit resident program for writers of fiction, resulting in a thesis and a Master of Arts degree in the teaching of writing; or a three-year, 63-credit program for writers of fiction, creative nonfiction, and plays, resulting in a book-length creative thesis and a combined degree of a Master in Fine Arts in creative writing and Master of Arts in teaching of writing.

PERKS: story workshop, *Hair-Trigger*, *F Magazine*, career nights, literary magazine seed money, writer-in-residence

NUTSHELL: One of the largest creative writing programs in the country, Columbia College's MFA seeks to prepare students for independent work as writers of publishable fiction, creative nonfiction, and plays, and for a wide variety of professions, such as journalism, theater, management, advertising, teaching, and law. The Story Workshop method, developed by John Schultz, informs each of the programs offered here—call them Plan A: MFA in creative writing; Plan B: MA in the teaching of writing; Plan C: combined degree. It focuses on helping the diverse students develop their own individual voices and provides a supportive, interactive, and challenging environment for developing their reading, writing, listening, speaking, critical thinking, and imaginative problem-solving capacities. Other opportunities include peer tutoring, Fiction Writers at Lunch mentoring program, study abroad in Prague, residence at the semester in Los Angeles program, tutor training, community outreach teaching, excellent internships, editing *Hair-Trigger* and *F Magazine*, annual career night, many graduate open mic and feature readings, and Story Week Festival of Writers.

Plan A students must have writing workshop and critical reading and writing courses, along with the thesis project. Plan B students need writing courses, practice with teaching and tutoring and electives in linguistics and pedagogical methods, along with the thesis project. Plan C includes all of the teaching credits, nine additional fiction writing credits, nine additional critical reading and writing courses, and six additional hours of thesis.

FACULTY: Randall Albers, Andrew Allegretti, Don DeGrazia, Ann Hemenway, Gary Johnson, Antonia Logue, Patricia Ann McNair, Eric Charles May, Joe Meno, Alexis Pride, John Schultz, Betty Shiflett, and Shawn Shiflett

Ann Hemenway, Director, Fiction Writing Department, Columbia College, Chicago, 600 S. Michigan Avenue, Chicago, IL 60605-1996, 312-344-7611, 312-344-8043, ralbers@colum.edu

Columbia College–Poetry
www.colum.edu

DEGREE: a two-year, 45-credit program for writers of poetry, resulting in a book-length creative thesis, a twenty-page craft paper, and a Master of Fine Arts degree in poetry

PERKS: *Columbia Poetry Review*, *Court Green*, poet-in-residence, visiting writers

NUTSHELL: The expectation of this program is that graduates will have a publishable book-length manuscript and be prepared to participate in the worlds of poetry, publishing, and the arts. The bulk of the credits are met in poetry workshops, craft seminars, and literature classes, but students will also take electives and attend a thesis seminar. The professors provide a knowledge of the history of poetry, in order to bring students up to date with the culture and imagination of poetry today. Sample classes include "Blur: A Craft Seminar in Hybrid Poetics," "Literary Collage and Collaboration," and "Women Romantic Poets." Visiting Poets have included Suzanne Buffam, Nick

Carbo, and Clayton Eshleman. Some experience in teaching is gained through graduate student instructorships and in editing both *Columbia Poetry Review* and *Court Green*, national literary magazines. Students benefit from the classes and meetings associated with the Distinguished Poet-in-Residence program.

FACULTY: Arielle Greenberg, Tony Trigio, David Trinidad, and Crystal Williams

DEFRAYING THE COST: Graduate Student Instructorships

David Trinidad, Director, Poetry Program, Columbia College, Chicago, 600 S. Michigan Ave., Chicago, IL 60605-1996, 312-344-8139, 312-344-8001, dtrinidad@colum.edu

Columbia University
www.columbia.edu/cu/arts

DEGREE: a two- to three-year, 60 credit resident program for writers of poetry, fiction, and nonfiction, resulting in a book-length creative thesis and a Master of Fine Arts degree in creative writing.

PERKS: New York City, CA/T program, *Columbia: A Journal of Literature and Art*, visiting editors and agents

NUTSHELL: A prestigious, competitive program that delivers its promise of producing talented and distinctive writers, The Writing Division at Columbia University is housed in The School of Arts and offers interaction with film, theater, and visual artists. A creative community of master teachers and gifted apprentice students, their workshops, seminars, and lectures are developed for writers by writers, with a practitioner's perspective on literature. Course subjects have recently included "Faces of War: Facts and Fictions" and "The Uses of Silence." This is one of relatively few graduate programs that regularly invites book editors and literary agents to campus to meet students. The program also prepares students for college-level teaching and for leading workshops in primary and secondary schools and in community-based organizations through the Columbia Artists/Teachers (CA/T) program. Students also get the chance to edit, manage, and publish their own national magazine, *Columbia: A Journal of Literature and Art*, as well as other informal publications, and to curate two reading series. Columbia takes pride in the successes of its students, with news on its website about the publications and prizes won by current and former students, and photos of their recent book covers. The university's location in *the* publishing city is not squandered: Students have access to events and internships at such institutions as the Poetry Society of America, the Academy of American Poets, *The New Yorker*, *The Paris Review*, and PEN American Center.

FACULTY: Lucie Brock-Broido, Nicholas Christopher, Timothy Donnelly, Austin Flint, Mary Gordon, Lis Harris, Richard Howard, Michael Janeway, Binnie Kirschenbaum, Richard Locke, Jaime Manrique, Ben Marcus, Patricia O'Toole, David Plante, Michael Scamma, Mark Slouka, Leslie Woodard, and Alan Ziegler

DEFRAYING THE COST: At the end of the first year, a small number of qualified students are awarded teaching assistantships from the Composition Program of Columbia College and the School of General Studies to begin the second year and continue into the third. These assistantships offer students experience teaching in the undergraduate Composition Program and provide a tuition credit for up to 11.5 points per term, along with a small cash stipend. Columbia is an expensive school, costing $17,435 for full residency. Financial aid is available. The Hertog Fellowship program enables six students a year to work as research assistants to writers who also serve as mentors, such as Rick Moody, A. M. Homes, Peter Carey, and Diane McWhorter.

School of Arts, Writing Division, Columbia University, 2960 Broadway, Room 415, New York, NY 10027, 212-854-4391, 212-854-7704, writing@columbia.edu

Eastern Washington University
www.ewu.edu

DEGREE: a two- to three-year, 72-92 credit resident program for writers of poetry and fiction, resulting in a written comprehensive exam, a book-length creative thesis, and a Master of Fine Arts degree in creative writing

PERKS: *Willow Springs*, EWU Press, Writers in the Community Project

NUTSHELL: The Inland Northwest Writing Center, in the literary city of Spokane, houses the MFA program and fosters creativity, diversity, and individual style, allowing students to fully explore their visions of writing, publishing, and teaching. Opportunities abound to give public readings at local bookstores, coffee shops, taverns, and clubs. Editing and publishing internships are available in the university's respected literary journal, *Willow Springs*, and with the EWU Press. It's a socially conscious program that teaches students to make creative writing accessible by volunteering as teachers, through the Writers in the Community Project, at area schools, correctional facilities, shelters, and other community organizations. This gives students a broad range of expertise when they graduate.

FACULTY: Jennifer Davis, Christopher Howell, Jonathan Johnson, John Keeble, Natalie Kusz, Gregory Spatz, and Nance Van Winkel

DEFRAYING THE COST: Incoming first-year students may apply for teaching assistantships that carry stipends and tuition waivers. Second-year students are eligible for merit scholarships and graduate assistantships.

Creative Writing Program, Eastern Washington University, 705 W. First Ave., Spokane, WA 99204, 509-623-4221, jjohnson2@mail.ewu.edu

Emerson College
www.emerson.edu/writing_lit_publishing

DEGREE: either a one-and-a-half-year, 40-credit resident program for writers of poetry, fiction, nonfiction, plays, and screenplays, resulting in a book-length creative thesis and a Master of Arts in publishing and writing, or a two-and-a-half-year, 52-credit resident program for writers of poetry, fiction, nonfiction, plays, and screenplays, resulting in a book-length creative thesis and a Master of Fine Arts degree in creative writing

PERKS: Boston, publishing internships, *Ploughshares*

NUTSHELL: The Writing, Literature, and Publishing program at Emerson offers an MA in publishing and writing for students who wish to pursue careers in publishing, and the MFA in creative writing for those who wish to pursue careers in the teaching of writing and literature. Both programs attend to the creative writer in the student, but the MFA is for writers in any of the creative media who are interested in a traditional academic writing program with courses aimed at developing writing style and artistic sensibility, and pursuing careers in writing fiction, nonfiction, plays, or screenplays. Boston is the other publishing city, and students in the publishing program can intern with publishers and agents, and get editing and production experience with the respected literary journal *Ploughshares*, founded by DeWitt Henry, and *Redivider*, run by graduate students.

FACULTY: Jonathan Aaron, Lisa Diercks, William Donohue, David Emblidge, Robin Riley Fast, Flora Gonzalez, Sarah Gore, DeWitt Henry, William Knott, Maria Koundoura, Uppinder Mehan, Pamela Painter, Donald Perret, Frederick Reiken, Murray Schwartz, Jeffrey Seglin, Don Skorczewski, John Skoyles, Dan Tobin, Jessica Treadway, Wendy Walters, and Douglas Whynot

DEFRAYING THE COST: There are options for low interest federal loans and federal work study, the Graduate MFA in Writing Scholarship, Bookbuilders of Boston Award, and the Rod Parker Playwriting Award, but the merit-based Presidential Fellowships and Graduate Assistantships do the most to defray costs. The Presential Fellowships are $10,000 tuition remission for the first year and an additional $3,000 for an additional semester. Recipients need not satisfy an on-campus work requirement. The Graduate Assistantships range from $3,000 to $5,000 per semester in tuition remission for the academic year and require recipients to work ten hours per week for thirteen weeks in academic or administrative departments.

Graduate Admissions, Emerson College, 120 Boylston St., Boston, MA 02116-1523, 617-824-8600. No direct e-mail. Fill out request forms on website for information to be e-mailed to you.

Fairleigh Dickinson University
www.fdu.edu

DEGREE: a two- to five-year low-residency program for writers of poetry, fiction, and creative nonfiction, resulting in a book-length creative thesis, an analytical essay, and a Master of Fine Arts degree in creative writing

PERKS: *The Literary Review*, visiting writers, study in England

NUTSHELL: This global program allows students to receive guidance from the international perspective of writers and poets throughout the world with its ten-day residencies at the Fairleigh Dickinson campus in Madison, New Jersey, in mid-August and the Wroxton College campus in Wroxton, England, in January. There are no grades, but rather a pass-fail system, and instead of traditional courses, there are four writing modules and one or two residencies each year. Modules last about ten weeks and are directed by a faculty mentor with advice from members of the cadre of global readers. At least five modules must be in the student's chosen genre, one must be in the craft of writing, and the rest are electives. Online workshops take place during the modules as well, so that students can comment on each other's work. A minimum of three residencies must be completed during the course of study. These comprise individual conferences with mentors and readers, group workshops, readings and instruction by distinguished visiting writers, student talks and readings, and other professional activities.

FACULTY: Renee Ashley, Walter Cummins, David Daniel, Linh Dinh, Martin Donoff, Fran Gordon, David Grand, Thomas E. Kennedy, Victor Rangel-Ribiero, Bino Realuyo, Renee Steinke, Laurie Stone, Terese Svoboda, and William Zander

DEFRAYING THE COST: Students defray the $10,200 annual cost of modules and residencies, plus travel, by working at jobs during the year. No other financial aid is available.

Director of MFA in Creative Writing, Fairleigh Dickinson University, The College at Florham, Madison, NJ 07940, 973-443-8710, writingmfa@fdu.edu

Florida International University
http://w3.fiu.edu/crwriting

DEGREE: a three-year, 48-credit resident program for writers of poetry, fiction, creative nonfiction, and screenwriting, resulting in a book-length creative thesis and a Master of Fine Arts degree in creative writing

PERKS: Miami/Fort Lauderdale, Annual FIU Writers Conference, FIU Literary Awards Competition, FIU Writers Workshop, Miami Book Fair, Writers on the Bay series, *Gulf Stream*

NUTSHELL: Founded in 1965 at the Biscayne Bay campus, this multi-ethnic, multicultural MFA is one of the top programs in the country. James Jones was once faculty here, and alumni have books with respected publishers. The Miami/Fort Lauderdale area is rich with Latin and Caribbean dance, theatre, art, and music institutions, as well as the Miami Book Fair every November. Students of this program take nearly as many classes in literature as they do writing workshops and have plenty of opportunities to learn about editing and arts administration with the university's literary journal, *Gulf Stream*; the FIU Literary Awards; the FIU Writers Workshop; and the FIU Writers Conference. The Writers on the Bay Series has brought to campus a broad range of writers such as Gay Talese, John Edgar Wideman, Elmore Leonard, and Rita Dove.

FACULTY: Lynne Barrett, John Dufresne, Denise Duhamel, James W. Hall, Campbell McGrath, Les Standiford, and Dan Wakefield

DEFRAYING THE COST: Tuition is $457 per credit for Florida residents and $771 per credit for nonresidents. That's $21,936 for Floridians and $37,008 for everybody else. Fellowships, tuition-remission scholarships, and teaching assistantships are granted on a competitive basis.

Les Standiford, Creative Writing Program Director, Florida International University, Biscayne Bay Campus, North Miami, FL 33181, 305-919-5857, standifo@fiu.edu

"Arizona State University is known for having a faculty of not only distinguished writers but distinguished teachers. It's one of the program's values. I have to say I didn't have any nightmare workshops. Everyone had a different style. Rios's workshops were more structured—he would sometimes give lectures or suggest revision exercises and strategies designed to get students thinking about other ways of approaching their work. Dubie ran his workshops more intuitively, with a strong focus on developing the individual poet's style. The other faculty members were somewhere in between. But all of the teachers focused on developing each student's work versus creating disciples."

—Mary Gannon, Editor, *Poets & Writers* magazine

University of Florida
www.english.ufl.edu/crw

DEGREE: a two-year, 48-credit resident program for writers of poetry and fiction, resulting in a book-length creative thesis and a Master of Fine Arts degree in creative writing

PERKS: agent and editor meetings, proximity to the Gulf of Mexico and the Atlantic Ocean

NUTSHELL: A small program founded in 1949 by Andrew Lytle, the editor of *Sewanee Review*, it features workshops that have nine students, maximum. The program expresses equal interest in writing workshops and literature courses but has no biases against any writing school or style. The instructors believe that criticism should "fill the design of the poem or story on its own terms." As well, they believe in helping writers with their careers, and invite ten agents, editors, and writers to visit the program each year to speak with students. Guests have included editors from *The New Yorker* and *New England Review*, the agent Jin Auh from The Wylie Agency, and authors Thomas McGuane and Anne Carson. Culturally rich Gainesville, Florida, has inexpensive housing and a leftover hippie subculture. The Gulf of Mexico and Atlantic Ocean are each about an hour away, in different directions.

FACULTY: Debora Greger, Michael Hoffman, David Leavitt, William Logan, Sidney Wade

DEFRAYING THE COST: Incoming MFA students receive half-time teaching assistantships equal to $9,200, to teach three courses over two semesters. They can also teach a fourth in the summer for an additional $2,900. In their second year, students can teach creative writing to undergraduates. These teaching assistantships come with tuition waivers. Supplementary fellowships for up to $2,000 can be added to the assistantship. And for the grand finale, one $30,000 alumni fellowship is awarded, with no teaching the first year.

Carla Blount, Program Assistant to the Director of Creative Writing, Department of English, University of Florida, P.O. Box 117310, Gainesville, FL 32611-7310, crw@english.ufl.edu

Goddard College
www.goddard.edu

DEGREE: a two-year, 48-credit low-residency program for writers of poetry, fiction, creative nonfiction, plays, screenplays, cross-genre work, and children's and young adult literature, resulting in a book- or production-length creative thesis, critical papers, and a Master of Fine Arts degree in creative writing

PERKS: Clockhouse Writer's Conference or Port Townsend Writer's Conference

NUTSHELL: Goddard is committed to self-directed education; the MFA is just one of its programs run on a distance learning model, and as of 2005, one of two in creative writing. While the very first low-residency MFA program was begun here by the poet Ellen Bryant Voigt in 1976, Goddard re-created it in the wake of the poet's departure to Warren Wilson in 1981. Now, you can choose the program either with brief eight-day residencies on the Goddard campus in Plainfield, Vermont, or in collaboration with Centrum Foundation at the Fort Worden State Park in Port Townsend, Washington. (The only way to experience both locales would be to request a transfer from one program to the other for the second year.) Only at Goddard in Vermont can you study children's and young adult literature. The summer residency in Fort Worden State Park is offered in sync with the Port Townsend Writer's Conference, and the summer residency in Plainfield overlaps the Clockhouse Writer's Conference, effectively doubling the workshop and guest writer opportunities. In either program, Goddard welcomes and encourages work in more than one genre and actively seeks out students of differing economic backgrounds, ethnic and racial groups, ages, and sexual orientations. The program teaches students to grow as writers, but also as critical thinkers and teachers. Students must complete fifteen hours in a teaching practicum in an area related to their future career plans.

FACULTY: Plainfield: Deborah Brevoort, Rebecca Brown, Maud Casey, Jan Clausen, Kenny Fries, Beatrix Gates, Elena Georgiou, Neil Landau, Leslie Lee, Jeanne Mackin, Douglas A. Martin, Nicola Morris, Richard Panek, Rachel Pollack, Rahna Reiko Rizzuto, Jacquelyn Reingold, Mariana Romo-Carmona, Sarah Schulman, Paul Selig, Alison Smith, Juliana Spahr, Darcey Steinke, and Jane Wohl

Port Townsend: Deborah Brevoort, Beatrix Gates, Jane Mackin, and Paul Selig

DEFRAYING THE COST: Financial aid is available.

Paul Selig, Director, MFA in Creative Writing, Goddard College, Plainfield, VT 05667-9700, 800-468-4888, admissions@goddard.edu

Goucher College
www.goucher.edu/mfa

DEGREE: a two-year, 36 credit low-residency program for writers of creative nonfiction, resulting in a one-hundred-fifty-page book-length creative thesis and a Master of Fine Arts degree in creative writing

PERKS: internships, agent and editor meetings

NUTSHELL: This is a single-genre, limited-residency program focused on the writing and publishing of personal essay, memoir, narrative nonfiction, literary journalism, travel/nature/science writing, biography, and professional writing over four semesters and three summer residencies. During the summer residencies on Goucher's scenic campus in North Baltimore, students attend writing workshops, craft lectures, seminars, and faculty and student readings, and are given career direction with editor and agent panels and trips to New York City to meet with top editors and agents. They also develop a contract of work for the upcoming semester. Each semester, students take one mentorship, which includes online discussions, required reading, writing about literature and the art and craft of creative nonfiction writing, and a corresponding course, and the contract includes a reading list, a correspondence method for packet exchanges, and a description of writing projects. Each spring semester begins with a structured online meeting or conference call. Students must also complete an internship of at least forty-five contact hours at a literary journal, a national or regional magazine, a daily or weekly newspaper, a recognized publishing house, or a Web-based publisher, or work with a published writer, agent, or editor. Past internships have been with *National Geographic* and the American Society of Journalists and Authors.

FACULTY: Thomas French, Diana Hume George, Philip Gerard, Kevin Kerrane, Lisa Knopp, Suzannah Lessard, Joe Mackall, Leslie Rubinkowski, and Richard Todd

DEFRAYING THE COST: It costs $565 per credit to attend, and $62.50 per night room and board during the summer residency, which means $20,340 for the complete study and $750 for each summer stay. There are no teaching assistantships or scholarships. However, if eligible, you may apply for a Federal Stafford Loan.

Patsy Sims, Director, Goucher College, 1021 Dulaney Valley Road, Towson, MD 21204, 410-337-6285, Mbell@goucher.edu

Hollins University—Children's Literature
www.hollins.edu/grad/childlit

DEGREE: a three- to four-year, 40-48 credit summer program for writers of poetry, fiction, or drama for children, resulting in a book-length creative or critical thesis, a comprehensive exam, and a Master of Arts or Master of Fine Arts degree in children's literature

PERKS: Francelia Butler Conference, writer-in-residence program, *Children's Literature Journal*

NUTSHELL: This is the only program that offers convenient, concurrent summer MA and MFA programs in the study and writing of children's and young adult literature. For six weeks every summer, a diverse community of scholars, writers, and distinguished writers-in-residence gathers here. Students may participate in an annual student-organized children's literature conference. MFA students will ground their creative work in the scholarly study of children's literature, and MA students may concentrate solely on the study of children's literature as a genre or ground it in creative writing. All students must pass a comprehensive exam to graduate, but the MA candidates must also show proficiency in a foreign language. Courses include "Children's Book Artists," "Minority Images in Children's Books," and "Gender and Identity in Science Fiction and Fantasy." GREs are not required. A distinguished writer or artist will be in residence for part of each term, and poets and writers will come to give lectures and readings. Students have opportunities to gain editing experience with *Children's Literature*, the journal founded in 1973 by the late Francelia Butler, a Hollins professor. Hollins also offers for writers of adult fiction and poetry a Master of Fine Arts degree in creative writing, and students of the children's literature program benefit from the course offerings.

FACULTY: Michelle Ann Abate, Brian Attebery, Susan Campbell Bartoletti, Rhonda Brock-Servais, Amanda Cockrell, Lisa Rowe Fraustino, Tina Hanlon, Len Hatfield, Alexandria LaFaye, Roderick McGillis, William Miller, Han Nolan, Julie Pfeiffer, Klaus Phillips, Ruth Sanderson, Karen Sands-O'Connor, J. D. Stahl, Karen Adams Sulkin, Ann B. Sullivan, C. W. Sullivan III, and Ernest Zulia

DEFRAYING THE COST: It costs $500 per credit, or $20,000 to $24,000 to earn the degree, plus the costs of room and board. Room and board costs $735 per six-week term in student apartments or dormitories. You can apply for student loans; Hollins occasionally grants partial tuition remission for qualified students.

Amanda Cockrell, Director, Graduate Program in Children's Literature, Hollins University, P.O. Box 9678, Roanoke, VA 24020, 540-362-6024, acockrell@hollins.edu

University of Houston
www.uh.edu/cwp/home.html

DEGREE: a three-year, 42 credit resident program for writers of poetry and fiction, resulting in a book-length creative thesis and a Master of Fine Arts degree in creative writing

PERKS: Inprint, Inc; *Gulf Coast*; visiting writers

NUTSHELL: This is a popular, high-ranking, and competitive program of study in literature and creative writing founded in 1979. (Note: There is a foreign-language requirement for admission.) The program admits ten new poetry and ten new fiction students each year and fosters a thriving literary community that helps to define the literary arts of Houston. Writing workshops, tutorials, literature courses, modern thought seminars, a thesis project, and electives make up the course study for the MFA. Most of the program's graduate students are awarded teaching assistantships to teach undergraduate classes and many also work with elementary and high-school students through the acclaimed Writers in the Schools program. As well, they gain valuable editorial and publishing experience as staff members of the student-produced, national *Gulf Coast* literary journal. The prestigious Margaret Root Brown Houston Reading Series, cosponsored by the nonprofit organization Inprint, Inc., presents seven readings each year, featuring some of the most important writers of fiction, poetry, and essays from around the nation and the world, including Salman Rushdie, Mario Vargas Llosa, Jhumpa Lahiri, Richard Russo, Sharon Olds, and Maxine Hong Kingston.

FACULTY: Robert Boswell, Chitra Divakaruni, Mark Doty, Nick Flynn, Kimiko Hahn, Tony Hoagland, Ruben Martinez, Antonia Nelson, Robert Phillips, Claudia Rankine, Daniel Stern, Adam Zagajewski, and, in conjunction with the School of Theatre, Edward Albee

DEFRAYING THE COST: Those eligible may apply for financial aid, and outstanding applicants may be nominated for Ehrhardt Fellowships and Mitchell Fellowships, for up to $10,000 to supplement their teaching stipends. The nine-month teaching assistantships provide health insurance, remit all tuition charges for up to nine credit hours each semester, and guarantee resident tuition rates for any additional credit hours. Graduate assistantships are for students who have reached the level of teaching sophomores. Inprint, Inc. awards $5,000 and $10,000 fellowships based on writing manuscripts. There are two Inprint/Michener Fellowships in honor of Donald Barthelme in poetry and fiction for $9,000 to $12,000. As well, there is the Brazos Bookstore/Academy of American Poets Prize and five Donald Barthelme Memorial Fellowships for $2,500. To ensure resident tuition for all its students, the Creative Writing Program awards $1,000 tuition fellowships to a limited number of returning students.

Creative Writing Program, Department of English, University of Houston, Houston, TX 77204-3015, 713-743-3015, cwp@uh.edu

University of Illinois–Urbana-Champagne
www.english.uiuc.edu/mfa/overview.htm

DEGREE: a three-year, 48 credit resident program for writers of poetry and fiction, resulting in a book-length creative thesis with author's preface, a public reading, and a Master of Fine Arts degree in creative writing

PERKS: *Ninth Letter*, eight million–volume research library

NUTSHELL: This young program, founded in 2002, aims to provide students with the pedagogical skills necessary to teach writing, extensive experience in literary editing and publishing, and a book-length, publishable manuscript. *Ninth Letter*, edited by Jodee Rubins, is the innovative literature and arts magazine publishing emerging and established writers and artists in a large format. The program offers a *Ninth Letter* publishing workshop each term and year- and semester-long assistantships for those interested.

FACULTY: Philip Graham, Tayari Jones, Brigit Pegeen Kelly, Laurence Lieberman, Michael Madonick, Audrey Petty, Richard Powers, Alex Shakar, Jean Thompson, Michael Van Walleghen, and David Wright

DEFRAYING THE COST: The tuition cost for attending the MFA in creative writing is $8,932 per semester including fees. Teaching Assistantships, Graduate College, and Departmental Fellowships offer tuition waivers in addition to the money received for teaching—$8,368.25 for one class a semester—or awards given—$1,000 to $15,000 for fellowships.

Steve Davenport, MFA in Creative Writing, University of Illinois–Urbana-Champagne, 210 English Building, 608 S. Wright St., Urbana, IL 61801, 217-333-3646, English-grad@ad.uiuc.edu

Iowa Writers' Workshop
www.uiowa.edu/~iww/

DEGREE: a two-year, 48 credit resident program open to writers of poetry and fiction, resulting in a book-length creative thesis and a Master of Fine Arts degree in creative writing

PERKS: *Iowa Review*, University of Iowa Press, Center for the Book, Educational Placement Office registration

NUTSHELL: Far and away the most famous writing program, "Iowa," as it's often called, was also the first creative writing degree program at an American university, and has been the model for those to follow. It is both a creative writing program that teaches writers how to teach—and thus make a living—and a writers' workshop that develops the potential of talented students into successful poets and fiction writers. Writing workshops, classes on genre forms, and literature seminars make up the basic requirements, with additional courses from the Translation Workshop, International Writers Workshop, Department of Theatre Arts, and visiting writers. Students learn how to teach college-level writing, and are encouraged to register in their last year with the Educational Placement Office for advance word on teaching jobs across the country. Iowa has educated many famously innovative, influential authors who have won Pulitzer Prizes, National Book Awards, and been U.S. poet laureates. In February of 2004, President George W. Bush awarded the school a National Humanities Medal—never before given to a university—and presented it to the program's longtime director, the late Frank Conroy. Conroy's successor, Lan Samantha Chang, was one of his students.

FACULTY: Marvin Bell, Ethan Canin, Lan Samantha Chang, James Galvin, Mark Levine, James McPherson, Marilynne Robinson, Cole Swenson, and Dean Young

DEFRAYING THE COST: There are $16,500 Teaching-Writing Fellowships for degree candidates entering their second year in the program; financial aid for a third of the students judged on the merit of their manuscripts; $7,665 one-quarter time Research Assistantships; $10,360 one-third time and $15,867 one-half time graduate teaching assistantships in the Liberal Arts College. Also, through the generosity of the James A. Michener Awards, poets and fiction writers with books near completion may receive $15,000 grants.

Lan Samantha Chang, Director, Graduate Program in Creative Writing, The University of Iowa, 102 Dey House, 507 N. Clinton St., Iowa City, IA 52242-1000, 319-355-0416, deb-west@uiowa.edu

---

"I went to Christopher Tilghman in a moment of crisis in the middle of my first semester, having been torched in a workshop and ready to quit the program. He said, very casually, 'Oh no—you belong here, don't do that,' and it was enough to keep myself 'up' until I finished. In my last semester, I connected with DeWitt Henry, who intuited what I was trying to do in my work when I couldn't articulate it well, and has supported me in various ways since. Emerson gave me teachers like Chris and DeWitt, Eileen Pollack, and Chris Keane, to point me to work I didn't know and time to read it all, plus the impetus to write regularly, which is all a writer ought to need, MFA or no. The degree itself gave me license to teach and that first experience you need to get jobs elsewhere. That part-time teaching—ten harsh years of it, off and on—combined with the editorial work I did on the *Beacon Street Review*, (now *Redivider*), gave me some experience when it came to *Night Train*, later on."

—Rusty Barnes, Founding Editor of *Night Train Literary Magazine*

Johns Hopkins University
www.jhu.edu/advanced/writing

DEGREE: a two- to five-year resident program for writers of poetry, fiction, general nonfiction, and science/medical writing, resulting in a book-length creative thesis and a Master of Fine Arts degree in writing

PERKS: Weekday evening and Saturday morning classes

NUTSHELL: This is a flexible, part-time program that offers a nurturing and demanding home for students to achieve their creative writing goals. Courses can be taken in Washington, D.C., or Baltimore, Maryland, in the evenings, on Saturday mornings, and in the summer. Students can move quickly and take three semesters a year and finish in two years, or take it slowly and finish in five years. This is a traditional education for writers who are unconcerned with writing trends. However, the program does offer courses that address the blurred border between fiction and nonfiction, and different styles in poetry. There are three core courses that are taken during the first year, which provide a foundation of form, technique, and reading. After this structured beginning, students enroll in writing workshops that allow them to create and revise their own projects. Courses include "Sentence Power: From Craft to Art," "Identity in Contemporary Writing," and "The Nature of Nature."

FACULTY: Stephen Bates, Mary Collins, Ellen Dudley, Mark Farrington, Ruth Guyer, Mary Knudsen, William Loizeaux, Paul Maliczewski, and Robert Schreur

DEFRAYING THE COST: Part-time students can apply for financial aid as well as scholarships from private sources and the State of Maryland.

Master of Arts in Writing Program, Advanced Academic Programs, Johns Hopkins University, G-1 Wyman Park Building, 3500 N. Charles St., Baltimore, MD 21218, advanced@jhu.edu

Johns Hopkins University—The Writing Seminars
www.jhu.edu/~writsem

DEGREE: a two-year resident program for writers of poetry and fiction, resulting in a book-length creative thesis and a Master of Fine Arts degree in The Writing Seminars, or a one-year resident program for science writers, resulting in a publishable thesis and a Master of Arts in The Writing Seminars

PERKS: visiting writers

NUTSHELL: The Writing Seminars, begun in 1947 by Elliot Coleman to blend the study and craft of poetry and fiction into a traditional liberal arts program, boasts many well-known graduates, including John Barth, Karl Shapiro, Russell Baker, David St. John, Cynthia McDonald, and Andrei Codrescu. The MFA degree is designed for students committed to the study and practice of literary writing at the highest level of accomplishment. Five poets and six fiction writers are admitted annually for continuous enrollment in workshops, forms courses, and literature electives. Here, genre-informed discussions, faculty conferences, independent readings of various texts, and interactions with visiting writers are emphasized so as to establish habits and skills necessary to lead the life of a writer. Visiting writers have included W. S. Merwin, Carol Frost, Julian Barnes, and Maxine Clair. The MA in science writing is a two-semester workshop and series of scientific press conferences. The first semester focuses on finding and defining science stories, and the second semester focuses on the thesis, which is either a publishable feature article or a series of essays. "Science Stories" are scientific press conferences followed by workshops on the particular ensuing story. The scope of these include the science, scientists' assessment of research results, scientific practice and malpractice, and the culture particular to that science. Journalistic principles are taught, and students learn to present science clearly, accurately, and seamlessly. Visitors have included Robert Coontz, editor of *Science*, and Corinna Wu from NPR.

FACULTY FOR MFA: Tristan Davies, Stephen Dixon, John T. Irwin, Alice McDermott, Jean McGarry, Dave Smith, and Greg Williamson

FACULTY FOR MA: Nell Boyce and Ann Finkbeiner

DEFRAYING THE COST: All students receive financial aid in the form of full tuition and a teaching assistantship, so they should show an aptitude for college teaching.

Graduate Admissions Coordinator, The Writing Seminars, Johns Hopkins University, Baltimore, MD 21218, 410-516-7563, regina@jhu.edu

Lancaster University
www.lancs.ac.uk

DEGREE: a two-year distance-learning program for writers of poetry, fiction, and scripts, resulting in a book-length creative thesis and a Master of Arts degree in creative writing

NUTSHELL: This program is run almost entirely through distance learning, except for the summer residency between the two years of study, with tutorial support through e-mail and computer conferences via the Web. A student is assigned a personal tutor who is an expert in the field. With every piece of writing the student sends to the tutor is a reflective commentary that the tutor will respond to. By the end of the course, this process accumulates as an invaluable resource of creative, critical, and reflective writing. The summer residency takes place at the university conference center and is visited by all MA tutors, as well as publishers and agents. Enrollment is biennial, in even-numbered years.

FACULTY: Linda Anderson and W. N. Herbert

DEFRAYING THE COST: It costs $1,550 per year in British pound silver, and while meals and accommodations are included in the summer residency, airfare is not.

Linda Anderson, Department of Creative Writing, Lancaster LA1 4YN, United Kingdom, +44(0)1524 594169, Landerson@lancaster.edu

Lesley University
www.lesley.edu/gsass/creative_writing/index.html

DEGREE: a two-year, 48 credit low-residency program for writers of poetry, fiction, nonfiction, and writing for young people, resulting in a book-length creative thesis, a craft lecture, and a Master of Fine Arts degree in creative writing

PERKS: Cambridge, The Art Institute of Boston at Lesley, Graduate School of Arts and Social Sciences, visiting writers, internships

NUTSHELL: One of the distinguishing characteristics of this otherwise typical low-residency program of four tutorial semesters at home and four ten-day Lesley residencies of workshops, classes, and events is the interdisciplinary component that encourages students to expand their abilities as writers by "widening the angles and deepening the fields of their vision" through work with faculty from The Art Institute of Boston at Lesley and by integrating their writing with such disciplines as art therapy, psychology, and education through Lesley's Graduate School of Arts and Social Sciences. Another distinction is the literary community of Cambridge, which includes bookstores, reading series, publishers, and writers. Paid or unpaid internships or assistantships in editing, publishing, and teaching have taken place at David R. Godine or Beacon Press, *The Harvard Review*, The Horn Book, Harvard Extension School, and Lesley University's Academic Resource Center.

FACULTY: Wayne Brown, Jane Brox, Teresa Cader, Rafael Campo, Pat Lowry Collins, Steven Cramer, David Elliot, Thomas Sayers Ellis, Tony Eprile, Laurie Foos, Indira Ganesan, Susan Goodman, Alexandra Johnson, Rachel Kadish, Michael Lowenthal, Rachel Manley, Kyoko Mori, Anita Riggeo, Christina Shea, and Janet Sylvester

DEFRAYING THE COST: Fees are broken down into semester fees, residency fees, and accommodation fees: $6,300 semester, $300 residency, and $500-$700 for accommodations. This will cost $26,400 for the program, and approximately $2,400 for accommodations. There is financial aid available.

Steven Cramer, Program Director, Low-Residency MFA in Creative Writing, Lesley University, 29 Everett St., Cambridge, MA 02138-2709, 617-349-8369 or 800-999-1959 x8369, jvanderv@mail.lesley.edu

Loyola Marymount University
http://bellarmine.lmu.edu/English/graduate.htm

DEGREE: a two-year resident program for writers of poetry, fiction, creative nonfiction, plays, and screenplays, resulting in a book-length creative thesis, a comprehensive exam, and a Master of Arts degree in English/creative writing

PERKS: Pacific Ocean, SYNTEXT

NUTSHELL: This program emphasizes the role that social justice plays in the practice of writing, and offers innovative courses that situate writing in wider and interdisciplinary contexts. They combine the canonical and the cutting-edge with classes in fiction, flash fiction, poetry, prose poetry, drama, surrealist techniques, journalism, ethnography, memoir, constraint-based writing, and screenwriting. The new SYNTEXT program offers students innovative ways to take writing into communities and landscapes and work for social justice in various ways. The beautiful campus sits on a bluff overlooking the Pacific Ocean in a friendly, safe part of West Los Angeles.

FACULTY: Greg Sarris, Chuck Rosenthal, Gail Wronsky, and Kelly Younger

DEFRAYING THE COST: There are graduate assistantships that pay, on average, $340 per week of 20 hours worked on-campus. There are also departmental scholarships and grants for those who apply for financial aid.

Paul Harris, creative writing Program Director, Loyola Marymount, Department of English, Loyola Blvd at West 80th St., Los Angeles, CA 90045-8215, 310-338-3018 (tel.), 310-338-7727 (fax), Pharris@lmu.edu

University of Massachusetts, Amherst
www.umass.edu/english/eng/mfa/mfaindex.html

DEGREE: a three-year, 54 credit resident program for writers of poetry and fiction, resulting in a book-length creative thesis and oral defense, and a Master of Fine Arts in English

PERKS: *jubilat, Crate, Massachusetts Review*, University of Massachusetts Press, Live Lit, visiting writers series, Juniper Literary Festival, Writers in the Schools, Hilltown Community Reading Series, Writers Work, The Jones Library/*jubilat* Reading Series and Poetry Book Group, Arts Administration Internship Program, Juniper Prize in Poetry, Juniper Prize in Fiction, Juniper Summer Writing Institute

NUTSHELL: Despite being an MFA in English, this is really one of the oldest and best creative writing programs, and offers a dynamic, rigorous program in an eclectic community. Writing workshops, private conferences, a few modern and contemporary poetry and fiction courses, the thesis project, and so many electives in literary history and aesthetics, interdisciplinary studies, publishing, arts administration, and the practice of teaching form this degree. This program offers its students a wide range of opportunities to participate in the writing life, including print and online literary journals *jubilat, Massachusetts Review*, and *Crate*; the University of Massachusetts Press and the Juniper book prizes it publishes in poetry and fiction; the student-run reading series, Live Lit, at Amherst Books; The Jones Library/*jubilat* Reading Series and Poetry Book Group, which pairs local and regional poets with others from across the country to discuss books; Hilltown Community Reading Series and Writers in the Schools outreach; The Writers Work forums, which bring in guests to discuss careers; the Literary Festival and Summer Writing Institute; and a visiting writing series that has entertained John Yau, Mary Caponegro, Barry Hannah, Tomaz Salamun, Charles Simic, and Eileen Myles. Amherst is near the Berkshire Hills and has a literary history that includes Robert Frost, James Baldwin, Emily Dickinson, and Robert Francis. Boston and New York City are both nearby if you need them.

FACULTY: Peter Gizzi, Noy Holland, Sabina Murray, James Tate, and Dara Wier

DEFRAYING THE COST: Everyone who is accepted to the program is sent an application for a teaching assistantship, which provides a stipend and full tuition waiver. There are other teaching positions available. Massachusetts residents get a discount on tuition.

Peter Gizzi, Director, MFA Program in English, University of Massachusetts, Amherst, MA 01003-9269, 413-545-0643, 413-545-3880, snape@english.umass.edu

Miami University
www.units.muohio.edu/english/gradcw/index.html

DEGREE: a two-year, 39 credit resident program for writers of poetry, fiction, and creative nonfiction, resulting in a book-length creative thesis and oral defense, and a Master of Arts degree in creative writing

PERKS: visiting writers, *Oxford Magazine*, Miami University Press

NUTSHELL: Another well-known, respected, and long-running writing program, Miami is small, with a faculty-to-student ratio of three to one. This tutorial atmosphere exists within a community of ambitious peers of national and international students in a small town forty-five minutes from Cincinnati. Half of the eight required courses are writing workshops where students are expected to write detailed critiques of one another's writing and present a revised portfolio of their own writing at semester's end. Both the University of Miami Press and the now online *Oxford Magazine* provide students with experience in editing and production.

FACULTY: Jeffrey Renard Allen, Steven Bauer, Annie Finch, Eric Goodman, James Reiss, Brian Roley, David Schloss, Kay Sloan, and Keith Tuma

DEFRAYING THE COST: Teaching Assistantships for $10,665, a summer stipend of $1,800, and tuition remission are available. Other assistantships make most classes funded. The Sinclair Award of $1,000 is given to the most promising student in each class.

Eric Goodman, Director of Creative Writing, Miami University, 501 East High St., Oxford, OH 45056, 513-529-5221, 513-529-1392, goodmaek@muohio.edu

University of Minnesota
www.english.cla.umn.edu/creativewriting

DEGREE: a three-year, 45 credit program for writers of poetry, fiction, and literary nonfiction, resulting in an exam, book-length creative thesis, and a Master of Fine Arts in creative writing

PERKS: internships with local presses and arts organizations, Split Rock Arts Program, visiting writers, awards, Minneapolis/Saint Paul

NUTSHELL: This program is for writers committed to pursuing the writing life and provides advanced graduate-level coursework in writing, language, and literature, as well as study in a related field. In the first two years, workshops in poetry, fiction, and literary nonfiction dominate, and classes on "Reading as Writers," as well as special topics of advanced study, let writers explore issues related to contemporary themes in American and world literature. The third year of study is devoted to the book-length creative thesis. Special topics in classes include "Spirit of Place" and "Reading as Writers: A Poetry Tour of Recent Winners and Finalists." Minneapolis/Saint Paul is a hub of literary small presses and arts organizations where students can intern. As well, the famed, interdisciplinary Split Rock Arts program offered by the university every summer gives students the opportunity to learn arts administration and attend weeklong workshops.

Visiting writers have included Charles Simic, Coleson Whitehead, Andrea Barrett, Adrienne Rich, and Vivian Gornick.

FACULTY: Charles Baxter, Michael Dennis Brown, Maria Damon, M. J. Fitzgerald, Ray Gonzalez, Patricia Hampl, Valerie Minor, Julie Schumacher, Madelon Sprengnether, and David Treuer

DEFRAYING THE COST: The program is committed to financial support for the full three years and has many fellowships and scholarships that provide salary or stipend, full tuition waiver, and subsidized health benefits.

Director of Graduate Studies, University of Minnesota, Department of English, 207 Lind Hall, 207 Church Street SE, Minneapolis, MN 55455, 612-625-6366, creawrite@unm.edu

University of Montana
www.umt.edu/grad/programs/english

DEGREE: a two-year, 45 credit resident program for writers of poetry, fiction, and drama, resulting in a book-length creative thesis, public reading, and a Master of Fine Arts degree in creative writing

PERKS: *Cutbank*, Second Wind Reading Series, visiting writers, Rocky Mountains

NUTSHELL: "A creative writing class may be one of the last places you can go where your life still matters," said Richard Hugo in his book

The Triggering Town. One of the earliest and most prestigious programs, begun in 1966 and shaped by Hugo, who traveled the country expounding on poetry's virtues, this MFA program continues to integrate creative writing with literature and turn out excellent writers, including Sandra Alcossar, Kim Barnes, Joshua Corey, Rick DeMarinis, Deirdre McNamer, and the late James Welch. Students may study both poetry and fiction, or just one genre. The national literary journal *CutBank* gives them opportunities to gain editing and magazine production experience. Courses in "Techniques of Modern Fiction" or "Traditional Prosody" are required. The student-run Second Wind Reading Series features poetry and fiction readings by local writers and students in the program. Missoula is a beautiful and diverse city of 60,000 in the Rocky Mountains with the Blackfoot, Bitterroot, and Clark Fork rivers running through it.

FACULTY: Judy Blunt, Kevin Canty, Debra Magpie Earling, Kate Gadbow, Patricia Goedicke, Joanna Klink, Deirdre McNamer, Greg Pape, and Karen Volkman

DEFRAYING THE COST: Teaching Assistantships pay $8,000 per year, plus tuition waiver, and are renewable. There are fiction and poetry awards given to outstanding writers in the program.

Kate Gadbow, Director, Creative Writing Program, University of Montana, Missoula, MT 59812-1013, 406-243-4652

"Emily Dickinson was a personal reason I applied, but professionally, I liked the three-year program with the literature reading emphasis. I was a foreign national at the time, and part of my goal was to spend as long 'in school' as I could on a student's visa. What the program at Amherst really taught me was how to read like a writer (and not a literary critic) and how to teach myself to write, and that I was the real and final judge of my own creative voice (i.e., an A in workshop doesn't make you a good writer). This came from living among a bunch of writers for three years in a close, intense experience. I had to ignore some of what I learned in order to find my own kind of voice. It also taught me that publishing wasn't a measure of quality, merely a measure of what that particular publishing world values. American publishing is by necessity very American, and ultimately, my real career was launched back home."

—Xu Xi, author of the novel *The Unwalled City*

Naropa University
www.naropa.edu

DEGREE: a two-year, 49 credit low-residency program or a two-year, 49 credit resident program for writers of poetry, fiction, creative non-fiction, performance, and translation.

PERKS: Summer Writing Program, Harry Smith Print Shop, Naropa in Prague

NUTSHELL: Both a resident MFA in writing and poetics and a low-residency MFA in creative writing are offered at Naropa, where in 1974 poets Anne Waldman and Allen Ginsberg founded The Jack Kerouac School of Disembodied Poetics. Students of the creative writing program take courses in both poetry and fiction, whereas single-genre study takes place in writing and poetics. Literary history and culture, and contemporary trends in literary theory are important to both programs. The Department of Writing and Poetics aspires to the classical Greek academia, a "grove" of learning where elders and students meet to explore traditional and innovative techniques and lore in the literary arts. Traditional and experimental approaches to writing are honored, as well as writing in performance, and the development of competent critical writing in both the literature courses and in the critical thesis requirement of the student's final manuscript. The new low-residency MFA in creative writing upholds the standards of the Writing and Poetics program, offering workshops, literature courses, and electives online during the year, and four-week residencies during the summer in Boulder to take advantage of the monthlong literary festival. Students of the low-residency program also get to share with their peers in the Writing and Poetics program during the summer. Each of the four weeks hosts a different set of guest faculty and workshops, exposing students to a broad range of issues in compositional craft and contemporary culture. Writing and Poetics offers courses in printing, bookbinding, and papermaking at Harry Smith Print Shop; it also teaches students to be literary activists in Project Outreach, and gives them a chance to take their spring semester at the Naropa in Prague program.

FACULTY: Keith Abbott, Reed Bye, Bobbie Louise Hawkins, Anselm Hollo, Laird Hunt, Bhanu Kapil, Andrrew Schelling, Eleni Sikelianos, Steven Taylor, and Anne Waldman

DEFRAYING THE COST: The resident program costs $615 per credit hour, plus a $250 student fee charge per semester or $120 summer fee. Boulder costs about $1,200 for room and board. For the low-residency program, graduate tuition is $615 per credit hour, plus a registration fee ($120 for summer, $250 for fall, $250 for spring). As well, there is a complicated array of technology fees: $60 for 1 credit;

$75 for 1.5 credits; $90 for 2 credits; $105 for 2.5 credits; $120 for 3 credits; $150 for 4 credits; and $180 for 5 credits. Financial aid is available, as are need-based Naropa Scholarships and merit-based $1,500 Engaged Writer Scholarships for study abroad. The program also offers a work-study program.

Admissions Director, Jack Kerouac School of Disembodied Poetics, Naropa University, Boulder, CO 80302. Fill out a request form on the website for information.

University of Nevada–Las Vegas
www.unlv.edu

DEGREE: a three-year, 42-54 credit resident program in writing and the study of literature for writers of fiction and poetry, resulting in a book-length thesis and a Master of Fine Arts degree in creative writing

PERKS: *Interim*, overseas study in a non-English-speaking country, the Peace Corps, International Institute of Modern Letters, *Popular Culture Review*, visiting writers series

NUTSHELL: A unique, internationally minded program with a student requirement to study in a non-English-speaking country, and with a partnership with the Peace Corps that allows students who wish to join both the Corps and the creative writing program to reduce the three-year residency to two and write their dissertations during their two-year commitment overseas. The creative writing program is at a metropolitan research university that creates bilingual, globally conscious fiction writers and poets, and prepares them for professional careers in publishing, teaching, and writing. Writing workshops, world literature courses, translation workshops, a semester or summer overseas in a non-English-speaking country, critical essay, and a book-length fiction or poetry thesis make up the basic three-year, 54 credit program. Those who participate in the Peace Corps Masters International Program need only fulfill 42 credits in Las Vegas, and will receive their MFA degree and resettlement allowance when the Corps commitment is complete.

FACULTY: Aliki Barnstone, Dave Hickey, Claudia Keelan, Douglas Unger, and Richard Wiley

DEFRAYING THE COST: The International Institute of Modern Letters offers graduate fellowships.

Douglas Unger, Director, International MFA Program, University of Nevada–Las Vegas, Department of English, Box 5011, 4505 Maryland Parkway, Las Vegas, NV 89154-5011, 702-895-3533, mfaunlv@unlv.nevada.edu

New England College
www.nec.edu

DEGREE: a two-year, 64 credit low-residency program with four semesters and five residencies for poets, resulting in a book-length manuscript and the award of a Master of Fine Arts degree in poetry

PERKS: free final residency, distinguished poets-in-residence

NUTSHELL: A poetry-only program that considers itself rigorous and peripatetic. The program fosters a close-knit, noncompetitive community when students gather for residencies in Heniker, New Hampshire, and aims to create better poets through a transformative study of creative writing and poetry. The program teaches students how to teach poetry at the secondary levels, read literary journals, and offer classes in the verse play and memorization and recitation. Student-to-faculty ratio is five to one, and communication during the semester occurs every three weeks and includes rigorous discussions on craft. Panel and craft lecture subjects during the residency periods have dealt with the poetry audience, the iambic line, translation, family poetry, experimental poetry, the light in Lucille Clifton's work, and the essentially erotic metaphor. Rolling admission, responses in two weeks, and no GREs are part of this program's efficient generosity, as well as the free-of-charge final fifth residency in which students present their final manuscript, give a lecture, participate in a senior panel, and give an extended reading. All the lectures and readings since 2002 are available on CD, CD-ROM, and MP3 formats.

FACULTY: Chard deNiord, Jeff Friedman, Judith Hall, Joan Larkin, Paula McLain, Anne Marie Macari, Jane Mead, Alicia Ostriker, F. D. Reeve, Ira Sadoff, Judith Vollmer, Anne Waldman, and Michael Waters; Maxine Kumin and Gerald Stern are distinguished poets-in-residence

DEFRAYING THE COST: The college offers financial aid through the Stafford Loan program, and all students who apply are immediately considered for annual, renewable, merit-based scholarships that relieve them of anywhere from $1,000 to the full cost of the tuition ($13,200). These are either The New England College Joel Oppenheimer Scholarship, named after the Black Mountain poet who taught at the college from 1982 to 1988, or The Gerald Stern Scholarship, named after the accomplished poet and current distinguished poet-in-residence at New England College. The school also offers the TMA Plan, a ten-month payment plan for any tuition costs not covered by financial aid. For the annual cost of $65, students can make monthly payments to Tuition Management Systems, which will allow them to spread out the cost of attendance.

Chard deNiord, Director, Creative Writing Program, New England College, Department of English, 7 Main Street, Henniker, NH 03242, 603-428-2252, graduateadmission@nec.edu

University of New Mexico
www.unm.edu/~english

DEGREE: a two-year, 34 credit residency program for writers of poetry, fiction, and nonfiction, culminating in a book-length manuscript for award of a Master of Arts degree in creative writing

PERKS: *Blue Mesa Review*, visiting writers series, Taos Summer Writers' Conference

NUTSHELL: Recently, a proposal has been made to the university to replace the MA program, begun at the dawn of graduate creative writing by Edward Abbey, with a three-year, 49 credit MFA. This would be a humanistic, academic program of literary history and writing workshops that gives students practical experience in publishing, arts administration, and teaching. Unlike the current MA, there would be no foreign-language requirement. Students can serve as editorial fellows on *The Blue Mesa Review* and assist with the planning and execution of the Taos Summer Writers Conference, which they can also attend.

FACULTY: Lisa D. Chavez, Joy Harjo, Gregory Martin, Daniel Mueller, Julie Shigekuni, Diane Thiel, and Sharon Oard Warner

DEFRAYING THE COST: Teaching Assistantships give students the chance to teach two sections per semester in the writing program in exchange for a stipend of about $1,150 to $1,250 per month and tuition remission up to twelve hours per semester. There are other grants and fellowships available.

Sharon Oard Warner, Director, University of New Mexico, Department of English, Humanities Building 229, MSC03 2170, Albuquerque, NM 87131, 505-277-6347, English@unm.edu

University of New Orleans, Lakefront
www.uno.edu

DEGREE: a two-year, 45 credit resident program for writers of fiction, nonfiction, plays, poetry, and screenwriting, resulting in a creative thesis and award of a Master of Fine Arts degree in drama and communications

PERKS: Tennessee Williams/New Orleans Literary Festival and its one-act play contest, *Bayou Magazine*, New Orleans

NUTSHELL: The degree is in Drama and Communications, but the writers attend the Creative Writing Workshop with its own faculty. It is an interdisciplinary program in imaginative writing with small workshops and plenty of electives. The school coedits and comanages with the University of West Florida the literary *Bayou Magazine*, which gives students an opportunity to work as editorial assistants. Then there's the fact that you are in the racially diverse, old French city of New Orleans, beloved by Tennessee Williams and William Faulkner, and home to great jazz and great food. The school brings in writers such as Richard Ford and Christopher Durang, Bobbie Ann Mason and Dana Gioia; teaches students how to teach at the university and secondary level; and offers students the chance to be first readers for the one-act play contest associated with the Tennessee Williams Literary Festival and attend the panels and master classes for free.

FACULTY: Frederick Barton, Randolph Bates, Carol Gelderman, John Gery, Steve Hank, Phil Karnell, Joanna Leake, Kay Murphy, and Dalt Wonk

DEFRAYING THE COST: A small number of Teaching Assistantships are available.

Director, The Creative Writing Workshop, University of New Orleans, New Orleans, LA 70148, 504-280-7454

Note: This listing was compiled before the catastrophic Hurricane Katrina hit New Orleans in late summer 2005. Please check with the institution concerning its restructured programs.

University of New Orleans Low-Residency MFA
www.uno.edu/lowres

DEGREE: a two-year, low-residency program for writers of poetry, fiction, nonfiction, plays, and screenplays, resulting in a Master of Fine Arts degree in creative writing

PERKS: online writing workshops and literature courses, monthlong European summer residencies

NUTSHELL: The first low-residency program to combine distance learning with study abroad in Madrid, Montpellier, and Brunnenberg, this program is also a departure from the now standard low-residency model. It features online workshops with other students during the semester, and monthlong summer residencies in Europe. This is not for the Luddite, but rather is perfect for students with late-model computers, Internet Explorer or Netscape Communicator version 5 or higher, familiarity with sending and receiving e-mail attachments—and a yen for travel. There's just no comparison for conversing with members of Ezra Pound's family at Brunnenberg, an alpine castle in Merano, Italy; taking a class on the key moments in French theater; and then attending the opera in Montpellier, France, or learning to translate great literature in Madrid, Spain, for the purpose of becoming a better writer. Of course, you can't be the regular low-residency student who holds down a day job and be able to take a month off every summer. Life is filled with little trade-offs.

FACULTY: Fredrick Barton, Amanda Boyden, Joseph Boyden, Moira Crone, John Gery, Peter Gizzi, Lee Gutkind, Rodger Kamenetz, Bill

Lavender, Hank Lazer, Deborah Meadows, Dinty W. Moore, Kay Murphy, Christine Pountney, Susan Schultz, and Michael Winter

DEFRAYING THE COST: The cost of two courses a semester, or 6 credits, is affordable at $2,754, but the summers abroad are about $3,800. You can apply for financial aid and scholarships.

Bill Lavender, Coordinator, Division of International Education, University of New Orleans, Metropolitan College, Box 582, New Orleans, LA 70148, 504-280-7247, wlavende@uno.edu

---

Note: This listing was compiled before the catastrophic Hurricane Katrina hit New Orleans in late summer 2005. Please check with the institution concerning its restructured programs.

The New School University
www.nsu.newschool.edu/writing

DEGREE: a two-year, 36 credit resident program for writers of poetry, fiction, nonfiction, and children's literature, culminating in a book-length manuscript for the award of a Master of Fine Arts degree in creative writing

PERKS: evening classes, summer writers colony, *LIT*, visiting writers series, the Writer's Life Colloquium

NUTSHELL: The New School has long entertained writers in workshops first developed in 1931 by Manhattan editor Gorham Munson, but it did not have an MFA program until 1996. It balances writing workshops with seminars in the reading of literature, and offers all courses in the early evenings Monday through Thursday to accommodate working students. All students must participate in The Writer's Life Colloquium, an ongoing colloquium of visiting writers, editors, writing teachers, publishers, and literary agents that reflects the school's belief that students benefit from exposure to many voices and genres. The literary journal *LIT*, founded by Mark Bibbins and edited by a new set of students each year, provides editing and production experience. The summer writers colony attracts additional writers from across the country. Overall, the program offers a staggering fifty public events every semester involving poets, biographers, essayists, novelists, critics, and publishers, to which all students are welcome.

FACULTY: Jeffrey Renard Allen, Hilton Als, Jonathan Dee, Elaine Equi, David Gates, David Hajdu, Fannie Howe, Shelley Jackson, Zia Jeffrey, Deborah Landau, James Lasdun, David Lehman, Philip Lopate, Harry Matthews, Pablo Medina, Honor Moore, Maggie Nelson, Dale Peck, Robert Polito, Liam Rector, Sapphire, Helen Schulman, Tor Seidler, Dani Shapiro, Laurie Sheck, Darcey Steinke, Benjamin Taylor, Abigail Thomas, Paul Violi, Susan Wheeler, and Stephen Wright

DEFRAYING THE COST: Tuition costs $8,750 per semester, plus $100 to register. There are federal and state loans and scholarships to help out.

Graduate Program in Creative Writing, New School University, 66 West 12th St., New York, NY 10011, 212-229-5630, nsadmissions@new school.edu

New York University
www.nyu.edu/fas/program/cwp

DEGREE: a two-year, 32 credit resident program for writers of poetry and fiction, culminating in a book-length manuscript for the award of a Master in Fine Arts degree in creative writing

PERKS: *Washington Square*, *Calabash*, visiting writers, culturally rich New York City, literary outreach programs

NUTSHELL: NYU is one of the best-known MFA programs for writers, and is one that focuses seriously and intensely on writing while offering students a distinguished core faculty and visiting faculty. The program is meant for writers who wish to teach, and is ideally completed in two years but will take longer for part-time students. The curriculum is composed of craft classes, workshops, a thesis, and electives from any of the university's departments or programs. The program is committed to developing innovative literary outreach programs that enable students to teach creative writing in both traditional and nontraditional settings, focusing on underserved and marginalized communities. These include programs that work with high-school students, hospital patients, and prison inmates. *Washington Square* literary journal, supported by the university, allows students to learn about editing and production. Visiting faculty members include such luminaries as Margaret Atwood, Robert Bly, Edwidge Danticat, Mark Doty, Edna O'Brien, and Michael Ondaatje.

FACULTY: Breytan Breytanbach, E. L. Doctorow, Galway Kinnell, Philip Levine, Paule Marshall, and Sharon Olds

DEFRAYING THE COST: The New York Times Foundation Creative Writing Fellowship pays five students stipends of $18,000, and NYU matches that grant with full tuition. Goldwater Writing Project awards six students $1,500 for a semester. The Starworks Foundation Project awards $3,000 to $18,000 and full tuition.

New York University, Graduate Program in Creative Writing,
19 University Place, Room 200, New York, NY 10003, 212-998-8816,
creative.writing@nyu.edu

University of North Carolina–Wilmington
www.uncw.edu/english

DEGREE: a five-year maximum, 48 credit resident program for writers of poetry, fiction, and creative nonfiction, resulting in a book-length creative thesis, an exam, and a Master of Fine Arts degree in creative writing

PERKS: publishing laboratory, visiting writers, Writers' Symposium

NUTSHELL: This program creates a community to support the writer through the solitary experience of being a writer. The department devotes itself to the pursuit of excellence in writing and includes dedicated educators who still believe in the value of art to the individual life and the collective culture. Students may enter this program to pursue the various career paths open to writers, or simply to master their own writing art. An equal number of credits (21) are required for writing workshops and literature or forms courses. Each year the program hosts a dozen visiting writers who teach for one week, one month, or entire semesters. The Writers' Symposium brings in renowned writers to meet with students in manuscript conferences, speak on panels, and give readings. These have included Andrea Barrett, Randall Kenan, Sebastian Matthews, and Tim Siebles. The Publishing Initiative allows students to takes courses in publishing and produce perfect-bound anthologies.

FACULTY: Barbara Brannon, Wendy Brenner, Mark Cox, Clyde Edgarton, Phil Furia, Philip Gerard, David Gessner, Rebecca Lee, Sarah Messer, Robert Siegel, and Michael White

DEFRAYING THE COST: The Philip Gerard Fellowship covers the cost of in-state tuition and fees for one MFA student per year; The New Scholar Award is a $1,000 grant awarded by the graduate school to a new MFA student each year; the Schwartz Scholarship covers the cost of in-state tuition and fees for an academically deserving student each year; and the Summer Research Grant is awarded to several students for $1,000 to cover summer research. There are also financial aid and teaching assistantships.

MFA Coordinator, Department of Creative Writing, University of North Carolina–Wilmington, Wilmington, NC 28403-5938, 910-962-7063, mfa@uncwil.edu

Northwestern University
www.english.northwestern.edu

DEGREE: a one-year, ten-course evening degree program for writers of poetry, fiction, and creative nonfiction, resulting in an independent master's project and a Master of Arts in creative writing

PERKS: internships

NUTSHELL: This evening-degree program offers professional development in the craft of creative writing to students who have day jobs and other daytime commitments through a workshop-based curriculum on the Evanston and Chicago campuses. Both full-time and adjunct faculty teach the ten courses and guide the students on their particular career paths of getting published, teaching, and editing. The ten courses are broken down into three workshops in the student's chosen genre, one cross-genre workshop, four relevant electives, a seminar on teaching creative writing and a seminar on the American publishing industry.

FACULTY: Anthony Adler, Michael Anania, Rebecca Bradway, Paul Breslin, Sheila Donahue, Reginald Gibbons, Susan Harris, Miles Harvey, Aleksander Hemon, Tara Ison, David Michael Kaplan, John Keene, Achy Obejas, Donna Seamon, Rone Shavers, Peggy Skinner, Sharon Solwitz, Neil Tessu, Anne Winters, and S.L. Wisenberg

DEFRAYING THE COST: As a part-time program for students with other obligations, including jobs, there are no teaching assistantships or graduate fellowships. However, students may apply for financial aid.

Cary Nathenson, Director, School for Continuing Studies,
Northwestern University, Evanston, IL 60208, 847-491-1545,
English-dept@northwestern.edu

Queens University of Charlotte
www.queens.edu/graduate/programs/creative_writing.asp

DEGREE: a two-year, low-residency program for writers of fiction, poetry, creative nonfiction, and stage and screen works, resulting in a creative thesis and the award of a Master of Fine Arts degree in creative writing

NUTSHELL: The program began in 2001 as a way to bolster the literary community of Charlotte. This low-residency program creates a close community with a student-to-faculty ratio of four to one, and a distance-learning component to the semesters at home. The focus of each semester is the writing workshop that begins during the seven-day residency and then continues online. Under the direction of a faculty leader, each student produces six submissions and must comment on the work received from the other two or three students in the workshop. Each residency in May and January includes panel presentations on professional issues, such as submitting to publishers and writing book proposals.

FACULTY: Jane Alison, Khris Baxter, Pickney Benedict, Cathy Smith Bowers, Ann Cummins, Jonathan Dee, J. D. Dolan, Major Jackson, Daniel Jones, Sally Keith, Helen Elaine Lee, Fred Leebron, Joanna Lessard, Andrew Levy, Rebecca McClanahan, James McKean, Daniel Mueller, Brighde Mullins, Naeem Murr, Jenny Offill, Alan Michael

Parker, David Payne, Susan Perabo, Robert Polito, Patricia Powell, Ron Rash, Katherine Rhett, Steven Rinehart, Elissa Schappelle, Peter Stitt, Elizabeth Strout, Abigail Thomas, Ashley Warlick, and Emily White

DEFRAYING THE COST: As with most low residency programs, Queens University of Charlotte's MFA allows for its students to work full-time to defray costs. Otherwise, Federal Stafford loans are available.

Fred Leebron, Director, Queens University of Charlotte, Department of English, 1900 Selwyn Ave., Charlotte, NC 28274, 704-337-2335, kobrem@queens.edu or matzj@queens.edu

Roosevelt University
www.roosevelt.edu/cas/sls/writing.htm

DEGREE: a two-year, 42 credit resident program for writers of poetry, fiction, and creative nonfiction, resulting in a book-length creative thesis and a Master of Fine Arts degree in creative writing

PERKS: Chicago, visiting writers, literary magazine production, *Oyez Review*

NUTSHELL: This program develops the student's literary knowledge and writing craft and offers real-world guidance in negotiating careers related to writing. It offers classes in poetry, fiction, creative nonfiction, and plays and screenplays, and courses in literary traditions, film studies, literary and critical theory, and the prevailing forces in the literary marketplace. Students are trained in one or more of the practical applications of writing, such as editing, publishing, and marketing, when they take the "Literary Magazine Production" class and produce the *Oyez Review*. They learn how to teach composition, literature, and writing in classes at Roosevelt or Chicago senior centers, and are given experience in public-service writing with internships in nonprofits or corporations. Chicago has a rich cultural and literary life, bringing area writers, such as Barry Silesky and Cris Mazza, into the classroom along with out-of-towners such as Alicia Ostriker and Orlando Ricardo Menes.

FACULTY: Mary Ber, Regina Buccola, Joe Fedorko, Ivor Irwin, Frank Rogaczewski, Lisa Stolley, and Janet Wondra

DEFRAYING THE COST: Roosevelt has financial aid through federal programs and the university-based graduate scholarship program. The Friends of American Writers, a literary organization founded in 1922 in Chicago, funds a scholarship awarded to an outstanding candidate admitted to the program. There are two graduate assistantships available through the School of Liberal Studies. A work-study position as assistant to the coordinator of the Creative Writing Program is available to students interested in arts administration, and individual Oyez Review internships carry a tuition waiver.

Janet Wondra, Coordinator, Creative Writing Program, Roosevelt University, 430 S. Michigan Ave., Chicago, IL 60605, 312-341-2157, jwondra@roosevelt.edu

WRITING WORKSHOP ETIQUETTE: CONSTRUCTIVE CRITICISM

MFA programs are small and often provide students with their main literary community. The use of phrases such as "this is a weaker moment" and "this passage is not as strong" may kindly disguise one's dislike of another's work, but delivering constructive criticism is even better. A good workshop should demonstrate that many routes lead to great writing, not just the ones you have been taking lately. Not synonymous with finding fault, constructive criticism gives the recipient confidence and provides ideas for how to improve, and helps the critic develop an open mind.

Every writing workshop is different, and each teacher should be the filter for discussions in the room, but each student must cultivate sensitivity. Your written comments about the manuscript do not carry your voice inflections, so be sure to make up for the loss of a friendly tone in your diction. This is especially true if you were quiet in the classroom and provide few reference points for the student who will read comments the next day.

To keep from feeling reticent, I recommend that you get to know the person behind the writing. Sharon Olds requires her NYU students to connect with others by going out on "poetry dates" at cafés and bars. This may be especially welcome when attending school in a metropolis, but anyone can feel alienated by the process of exposing and editing creative writing, not least of all the students who have been out of the classroom for years. Workshop etiquette is just like good manners anywhere—make others feel at ease, and don't say anything to others you wouldn't like said to you.

Sarah Lawrence College
www.slc.edu

DEGREE: a two- to three-year, 36 credit resident program for writers of poetry, fiction, and creative nonfiction, resulting in a book-length creative thesis and a Master of Fine Arts degree in creative writing

PERKS: Community Writers Program, *Lumina*, nearby New York City, writer-in-residence

NUTSHELL: In tandem with the philosophy of the college, the MFA emphasizes individual development in a noncompetitive environment. Students' work is paid close attention in biweekly conferences with the faculty member teaching each semester's workshop, and only one elective. Encouraged to study with various teachers, students can also take master classes with the writer-in-residence. Faculty members educate students on the basics of publishing and encourage them to help out at the student-run literary journal *Lumina*. As well, teaching experience is gained through the Community Writers Program, with placement at community centers, elementary schools, senior centers, and correctional facilities. This is a popular, beloved program situated in a leafy suburb thirty minutes from the literary scene of downtown Manhattan by nearby train. But at Sarah Lawrence, the students form a tight-knit community like no other, and engage each other in discussions, readings, and community gatherings. The 36 credits of coursework do not include the thesis, and can be spread out over three years for part-time students. The first year, students take an elective course, two semester workshops, and two reading courses. The second year consists of only two workshops and the thesis, so that writing is the focus.

FACULTY: Jo Ann Beard, Laure-Anne Bosselaar, Kurt Brown, Melvin Jules Bukiet, Rachel Cohen, Stephen Dobyns, Carolyn Ferrill, Susan Gardinier, Myra Goldberg, Joshua Henkin, Kathleen Hill, Marie Howe, Kate Knapp Johnson, William Melvin Kelley, Michael Klein, Mary LaChapelle, Joan Larkin, Paul Lisicky, Thomas Lux, Mary Morris, Brian Morton, Dennis Nurkse, Stephen O'Connor, Grace

Paley, Kevin Pilkington, Lucy Rosenthal, Vijay Seshadri, Joan Silber, and Penny Wolfson

DEFRAYING THE COST: Financial aid is available to those who are qualified.

Susan Guma, Dean of Graduate Studies, Graduate Studies, Sarah Lawrence College, Bronxville, NY 10708, 914-395-2371, sguma@mail.slc.edu

Seattle Pacific University
www.spu.edu/mfa

DEGREE: a two-year, 64 credit low-residency program of four semesters and five ten-day residencies for writers of poetry, fiction, and creative nonfiction, culminating in the completion of a book-length manuscript, delivery of a lecture and public reading, and the award of a Master of Fine Arts degree in creative writing. **Note:** If studying two genres instead of one, the program becomes three years.

PERKS: *Image: A Journal of Arts and Religion*, Milton Center conference, Glen Workshop in Santa Fe

NUTSHELL: This program is for writers centered in their faith who are interested in writing within the context of Judeo-Christian faith without being didactic, sectarian, or sentimental. Think Augustine, Dante, Milton, Dostoevsky, T. S. Eliot, Flannery O'Connor, Walker Percy, and Annie Dillard. The master and apprentice model is well translated in the largely contemplative and solitary low-residency program of correspondence semesters of creative writing projects, reading lists, and critical papers, and the ten-day workshop/craft class/lecture residencies. The difference is that students don't go to Seattle Pacific University but instead attend the theme-based Glen Workshop in August at St. John's College in Santa Fe, New Mexico, and Camp Casey on Whidbey Island, Washington, on Puget Sound, in March. Director Gregory Wolfe is the founder and editor of the respected literary journal *Image: A Journal of Arts and Religion*, which sponsors a Milton conference and the Glen Workshop, and invites visiting writers, artists, and musicians along to the residencies. The 2005 theme for Glen was "This Great Unknowing: Drawing Near to Mystery." By the end of the two years, students will have read fifty to sixty books.

FACULTY: Robert Clark, Leslie Layland Fields, Paul Mariani, and Gregory Wolfe

DEFRAYING THE COST: Tuition is around $11,800 for the first and second year, and $2000 for fifth residency. There is financial aid, and federal and state work-study are available.

Gregory Wolfe, Director, Seattle Pacific University, 3307 Third Ave. West, Seattle, WA 98119, 206-281-2109, mfa@spu.edu

Spalding University
www.spalding.edu

DEGREE: a two-year low-residency graduate program of four semesters and five residencies for writers of fiction, poetry, creative nonfiction, children's literature, and plays and screenplays, resulting in a complete book-length thesis and a Master of Fine Arts degree in writing

PERKS: The Book in Common, *The Louisville Review*, visiting writers program, cross-genre opportunities

NUTSHELL: Sena Jeter Naslund prefers the more grammatically correct term "brief residency" to describe her new program, and believes that it is superior to the traditional resident graduate programs because "the process of writing is not continuously interrupted by attending classes." Each semester, Naslund selects a contemporary "Book in Common" in one of the five areas of concentration for all students and faculty to read. During the first week of the ten-day residency, everyone gathers to discuss the book, meet with its author, and complete cross-genre writing assignments. Here, it is believed that writing is writing and there are qualities to be learned from each area of concentration that can be applied to every other area, such as the vividness and compactness of language in poetry informing fiction, creative nonfiction, writing for children, playwriting, and screenwriting. The rest of the semester is spent in one-on-one correspondence with a faculty mentor on a personally designed study plan. The faculty are excellent teachers and writers who continue to publish. Each has only five students per semester.

FACULTY: Dianne Aprile, Rane Arroyo, Susan Campbell Bartoletti, Julie Brickman, Louella Bryant, Richard Cecil, Mary Clyde, K. L. Cook, Debra Kang Dean, Kathleen Driskell, Bob Finch, Connie Mae Fowler, Charles Gaines, Kirby Gann, Richard Goodman, Roy Hoffman, Silas House, Claudia Hunter Johnson, Robin Lippincott,

Joyce McDonald, Cathleen Medwick, Maureen Morehead, Sena Jeter Naslund, Elaine Orr, Greg Pape, Linda Busby Parker, Molly Peacock, Melissa Pritchard, Jeannie Thompson, Neela Vaswani, Luke Wallin, Mary Yukari Waters, Brad Watson, Crystal Wilkinson, and Sam Zalutsky

DEFRAYING THE COST: The first three semesters each cost $5,040; the last semester, with its two residencies, costs $5,640. Prospective students can apply for student loans, or either of the $500 to $1,000 MFA in Writing Scholarship Fund for Minorities or the MFA in Writing Scholarship Fund. Graduate Assistantships will cut one-fourth to one-third of the tuition cost and give you the opportunity to work in the writing center, on the *Louisville Review* newsletter, or in the MFA office. Expect $153 to $680 per residency in accommodations if you go with what they provide, as much as $250 for new books, $200 for postage when sending packets, parking fees if you drive to the school, a $150 graduation fee, and a $100 creative thesis fee. Don't forget to check your local library and used bookstores at home or online, and check out the bookshelves of well-read family members and friends to reduce the cost of texts.

Sena Jeter Naslund, Director, Creative Writing Program, Spalding University, 851 S. Fourth St., Louisville, KY 40203, 502-585-9911 ext. 2423 or 800-896-8941 ext. 2423, mfa@spalding.edu

University of Texas–Austin
James A. Michener Center for Writers
www.en.utexas.edu

DEGREE: a three-year resident interdisciplinary program for writers of poetry, fiction, plays, and screenplays, resulting in a creative thesis and the award of a Masters of Fine Arts degree in creative writing

PERKS: Harry Ransom Humanities Research Center, University of Texas English department, the music city of Austin

NUTSHELL: This is a close-knit program that admits about a dozen students each year and requires them to be writers of multiple genres—at least two—while they explore new forms and voices and develop a body of work in a primary field. Every student receives a fellowship with a stipend so that no one needs to stress about teaching or the regular coursework, and students need not compete for resources. Course requirements are flexible enough for students to shape their own curricula, and a new pilot Writers' Outreach Program is under way for students to create and implement community writing workshops for course credit. Austin, Texas, is often cited as one of the most livable cities in the country. The interdisciplinary program is housed next to the main campus of the University of Texas in the J. Frank Dobie home—a Texas historic landmark on the National Register of Historic Places—where Dobie, a folklorist, novelist (the writer of *Apache Gold and Yaqui Silver*), and UT professor from 1914 to 1947, held backyard literary salons into the early 1960s. Michener MFA students have access to all the resources of the university's English department (where there is another graduate creative writing program) and libraries, including the Harry Ransom Humanities Research Center, which houses archives of major playwrights, Hollywood producers, and American authors, from Tom Stoppard to David O. Selznick to D. H. Lawrence. Visiting professors across the genres include Ben Marcus, Joy Williams, Heather McHugh, Tino Villanuevo, Ann Rapp, and Emily Tracy.

FACULTY: Michael Adams, Robert Foshko, Laura Furman, Zulfikar Ghose, Stephen Harrigan, Elizabeth Harris, Kurt Heinzelman, Rolando Hinojosa-Smith, Judith Kroll, Peter LaSalle, James Magnuson, Ruth Margraff, Khaled Mattawa, Charles Ramirez-Berg, James Still, David Wevill, Thomas Whitbread, and Susan Zeder

DEFRAYING THE COST: Each student admitted to the program receives a fellowship of $20,000 as of September 2005 from the endowment of James A. Michener and Mari Sabusawa Michener, which includes a remission of tuition and fees and can be renewed in subsequent years with the recognition of the student's progress. Professional development funds also available.

James Magnuson, Director, Michener Center for Writers, University of Texas–Austin, 702 East Dean Keeton St., Department of English, Austin, TX 78712-1164, 512-471-4991, mcw@www.utexas.edu

University of Texas–El Paso
www.utep.edu

DEGREE: a three-year, 48 credit resident program for writers of poetry, fiction, nonfiction, plays, and screenplays, culminating in a book-length creative thesis and the award of a Master in Fine Arts degree in creative writing of the Americas

PERKS: *Rio Grande Magazine*, MFA Student Organization

NUTSHELL: This is the only bilingual MFA program in the country—with English and Spanish speaking options—and it offers an experience of close mentoring, with an emphasis on placement in careers in teaching, editing, and writing. MFA students come from all over Latin America and the United States and can study literary translation, libretto writing, border culture, novella, and the prose poem. They can also attend literature classes offered by theater, English and language departments, and see their work produced on stage in collaboration with the Musical Theater Department. Situated in the Chihuahuan Desert where Mexico and the United States meet, the MFA program explores the linguistic and literary traditions of the Americas. Since Hispanics are now a "majority-minority" in the U.S., this program seeks to equip writers of any ethnicity and origin with the skills needed to approach the bilingual workforce. The MFA Student Organization acts as a Welcome Wagon to incoming students, arranging reading venues, supporting their needs and concerns at faculty/staff meetings, and assisting with modest funds for those presenting student papers at conferences. Students have gone on to win international literary prizes. Visiting writers have included Elena Poniatowska, James Navé, and Sara Anson Vaux.

FACULTY: Rosa Alcalá, Daniel Chacón, Johnny Payne, Luis Arturo Ramos, Benjamin Alíre Sáenz, Leslie Ullman, Lex Williford

Johnny Payne, Creative Writing Program Director, University of Texas–El Paso, El Paso, TX 79968, 915-747-5713, Jpayne@utep.edu

Vermont College
www.tui.edu/vermontcollege

DEGREE: a two-year low-residency program for writers of poetry and fiction for children and young adults, resulting in a book-length creative thesis, lecture, public reading, and a Master of Fine Arts in writing for children and young adults

NUTSHELL: All Vermont College programs are low-residency, and the regular MFA in creative writing, begun in 1981, is part of the original trio of such graduate degrees. Vermont College was acquired by the Ohio-based Union Institute & University, but continues to exist in Montpelier and Brattleboro, Vermont. The MFA in writing for children and young adults was established in 1997 and demands rigorous academics during the semester to counterbalance the camaraderie and stimulation of other writers during the eleven-day residencies. The students are a mature and focused group of writers. Residencies convene in January and July and include workshops; lectures; readings; special presentations by visiting writers, editors, and publishers; and semester-planning components. Workshops have ten to twelve students and are conducted by two faculty members, providing a forum rich with creative tension and that invites active dialogue on issues of craft, style, and aesthetics. The first and second semesters concentrate mainly on writing, reading, and critical thinking. The third semester adds to that a twenty- to fifty-page critical thesis. In the fourth semester, a book-length manuscript of writing is completed, and both a lecture and a reading are presented at the final residency.

FACULTY: M. T. Anderson, Kathi Appelt, Marion Dane Bauer, Margaret Bechard, Carolyn Coman, Sharon Darrow, Louise Hawes,

Ellen Howard, Lisa Jan-Clough, Liza Ketchum, Ron Koertge, Laura Kvasnosky, Ellen Levine, Alison McGhee, Norma Fox Mazer, Phyllis Root, Jane Resh Thomas, Tim Wynne Jones

DEFRAYING THE COST: Each semester costs $5,780, room and board is $650, and the technology fee is $57. This comes to $26,598. There are merit- and diversity-based scholarships generously donated by both private sources and publishers such as Houghton Mifflin, Harcourt, Penguin Group (USA) Inc., and Candlewick Press. Financial aid is also available.

MFA in Writing for Children and Young Adults, Vermont College, Montpelier Campus, 36 College St., Montpelier, VT 05602, 800-336-6794. For information to be e-mailed, fill out a form on their website

Warren Wilson College
www.warren-wilson.edu

DEGREE: a two-year low-residency program with four semesters and four residencies for writers of poetry and fiction, culminating in a book-length manuscript and public reading for the award of a Master in Fine Arts degree in creative writing

NUTSHELL: This is the wolf from which all low-residency MFA programs descend. Designed and begun by the poet, Ellen Bryant Voigt at Goddard College in 1976, this first low-residency MFA in creative writing, designed for students who wish to continue working at their jobs and living with their families at home, was transferred to Warren Wilson College in 1981 as its only graduate division. Students send packets of creative writing and book reports every three weeks to their faculty adviser, usually working twenty-five hours a week, and then spend ten days every six months in Asheville for craft classes, writing workshops, and readings. The ten-day residency closes a non-resident semester and initiates another, and is where a close-knit community is developed. By the time they graduate, each student will have written an analytical paper, read fifty to eighty books, taught a class to fellow students, given a public reading of his or her work, and prepared a manuscript of fiction or poetry. Recent residency class and lecture topics include "The Breakout Moment: Unpredictability in the Novel" and "Is It Poetry? Is It Prose? Does It Matter?"

FACULTY: Elizabeth Arnold, Karen Brennan, Lan Samantha Chang, Charles D'Ambrosio, Laura Kasischke, Heather McHugh, Steve Orlen, Martha Rhodes, Peter Turchi, and Ellen Bryant Voigt

DEFRAYING THE COST: There is the Holden Minority Scholarship that awards full tuition and residency fees for the entire degree program, and through the Federal Stafford Loan program options for an MFA Grant and the Eric Mathieu King Scholarship for one year, renewable.

Peter Turchi, Director, MFA Program for Writers, Warren Wilson College, P.O. Box 9000, Asheville, NC 28815-9000, 828-771-3715 (tel.), 828-771-7005 (fax)

Wichita State University
www.wichita.edu

DEGREE: a two-year, 48 credit resident program for writers of poetry and fiction, resulting in a book-length creative thesis, a written comprehensive exam, and a Master of Fine Arts degree in creative writing

PERKS: distinguished visiting writer tutorials

NUTSHELL: This is one of the oldest programs in the country and is respected for producing well-trained writers and well-prepared teachers of writing and literature. The emphasis is on the development of skills and understanding in the practice of imaginative writing and on related academic study. The basic program is heavier on literature courses than on writing workshops, but once a semester students may enroll in a one-month tutorial with a visiting poet or fiction writer to work in one-on-one conferences.

FACULTY: Margaret Dawe, Albert Goldbarth, Jeannine Hathaway, W. Stephen Hathaway, Philip Schneider, and Richard Spilman

DEFRAYING THE COST: A majority of students hold teaching assistantships for all or part of their residence, which gives them a full waiver of tuition and fees. The Department of English also awards creative writing fellowships to three outstanding MFA teaching assistants.

Philip Schneider, Director of Creative Writing, Wichita State University, Department of English, 1845 N. Fairmount, Wichita, KS 67260-0014, 316-978-3130, Philip.Schneider@wichita.edu

University of Wisconsin, Madison
http://creativewriting.wisc.edu

DEGREE: a two-year, 36 credit resident program for writers of poetry, fiction, and creative nonfiction, resulting in a book-length creative thesis and a Master of Fine Arts degree in creative writing

PERKS: *Madison Review*, *Canvas*, University of Wisconsin Press, George B. Hill and Therese Muller Memorial Creative Writing Contest, The Charles M. Hart Writers of Promise Awards, Eudora Welty Fiction Thesis Prize, Felix Pollack Poetry Thesis Prize, August Derleth Prize, writer-in-residence

NUTSHELL: A small program admitting poets and fiction writers in alternate years, with twelve students overall in any two year period, Madison teaches students in both writing and teaching, and offers them money at every turn. Besides the teaching assistantships and fellowships, there are writing awards and contests for individual stories and poems, and for thesis projects. Editing and publishing opportunities abound with the *Madison Review* and The University of Wisconsin's respected book contests, The Brittingham Prize for Poetry and the Felix Pollack Prize for Poetry. In addition, the Wisconsin Institute writer-in-residency program brings a post-MFA writer to campus to lead a workshop and read from a work-in-progress.

FACULTY: Amy Quan Barry, Heather Dubrow, Roberta Hill, Amaud Jamaul Johnson, Jesse Lee Kerchival, Richard Knowles, Ron Kuka, Judith Claire Mitchell, Lorrie Moore, Rob Nixon, and Ron Wallace

DEFRAYING THE COST: Two poets are awarded Martha Meier Renk Distinguished Graduate Fellowships in Poetry, which provide $15,000

stipends, $1,500 expense accounts, and health benefits during one of their two years in residence and a teaching assistantship in the other. All other students receive two-year teaching assistantships that include an $8,500 annual stipend the first year and $9,000 the second, free tuition, health benefits, and extensive teacher training. As well, everyone but the poetry Renk fellows receive $2,500 Renk, Dorothy D. Bailey, or Anastasia C. Hoffman Prize scholarships at the end of their first year in residence. Teaching assistants teach one introductory creative writing course each semester of their first year, and one introductory composition course each semester of their second year.

Ron Wallace and Jesse Lee Kerchival, Codirectors of Creative Writing, The Program in Creative Writing, Department of English, Helen C. White Hall, 600 N. Park St., University of Wisconsin–Madison, Madison, WI 53706, 608-263-3750, english@wisc.edu

4 Colonies and Residency Programs

A character in *Urban Bliss*, a novel by Janice Eidus, is a composer of microtonal music, a genre unfamiliar to the author before her enjoyable dinner conversations with a modern composer at MacDowell Colony. Prose writer Destiny Kinal found that her visits to the visual artists' studios at the intimate Saltonstall Arts Colony opened "a particular sensory door to my creativity," leading her not only to collaborate with artists herself but also to share the discovery by developing a series of collaborative workshops involving artists, writers, and letterpress book artists in Montolieu, France. While in residence at Civatella Ranieri, poet Denise Duhamel visited the local Umbrian churches and was inspired to write a poem in the form of a fresco. All of these writers went away to write and ended up venturing outside their usual perspectives into new creative territory.

The artist colony is a partly told secret in the literary community—well-known to some, unknown to others, and misunderstood by writers who think they can (or should) do without. But nearly all writers have found themselves accepting the marginal status of their vocation by writing in their spare time—after the chores are done, the day job complete, the children bathed and in bed, the phone calls and e-mails answered, the friends and lovers satisfied. Rather than rely entirely on dawn or midnight appointments with their typewriters, computers, or journals to work, poets, novelists, playwrights, short-story writers, essayists, and narrative nonfiction writers could instead spend full weeks and months releasing the muses and getting their writing done.

If you have ever been transported by Aaron Copeland's *Appalachian Spring* or traveled far from the confines of your couch with Henry Thoreau or John Muir, then you know how wilderness can inspire and invite us. Consider that Thomas Moran, who loved the Buffalo River in the Ozarks, painted images of Yosemite that were so inspiring that Congress decided to create a national park to preserve its beauty for future generations. In 1984, the Rocky Mountain National Park felt it was high time to repay the debt to the artists, writers, and composers who brought the natural world to spectacular life and visitors to the parks; they created the first artist-in-residence program in a national park. Certainly Anne McCrary Sullivan, a poet who teaches the poetics of science, has benefited from this decision. A colony creates a community of people, but a residency in a park pulls in a different sort of crowd: Sullivan was enriched from a few weeks with the herons, anhingas, and hawks as an Artist-in-Residence in the Everglades (AIRIE).

There are quite a few ranches, farms, and castles converted to colonies and residency programs. You can stay somewhere that caters to you completely, or stay, as I did in the spring of 1989, at a colony that requires you to pay for your own food and cook your meals. That idyll in the mountains near San Diego was called Dorland Mountain Arts Colony, and it had as many as seven residents at a time. My group (a watercolorist, a poet, a gourd sculptor, a novelist, and a composer), all met in the uninhabited—except for the field mice and alligator lizards—kitchen house every Sunday for pot luck suppers and to play the game of dictionary using magnificent, old, leatherbound books. The experience rewired my mind to be receptive at any hour of the day to the muse, especially daylight hours up on the ridge, while sitting in a red Adirondack chair facing the mountains and being watched over by Shady, a wolf-shepherd mix. I'd been so worried before I got there about rattlesnakes, which were nowhere to be found, and once there I was unnerved by the darkness in my cabin without electricity, and startled by the acoustics of ground-nesting birds, squirrels on the roof, and deer rubbing against my little orchard house, that it never occurred to me that a brushfire could sweep up the desert mountainside of Southern California and claim the colony. But in 2004 that happened. They are trying to rebuild, but it will be a different Dorland, no less beautiful in its trails and vistas, but without the history of its founders and the writers, painters, composers, sculptors, and photographers who were supported there.

If you have never had the extraordinary experience of having nothing to do but write, no chores, no responsibilities, no guilt or interruptions, then you should. The flow you eventually get often carries you past your destination into whole new projects, different genres, collaborations. I say "eventually" because the adjustment to the new environment and exciting opportunity can slow the start of this flow. You may write a few letters the first few days; take long walks; gaze at the sea, mountains, prairie, rivers, or lakes; and read. This is fine—don't panic. You are acclimating to your new surroundings and new people, ridding yourself of the city, or traffic lanes, or even getting rid of jet lag. This is part of the experience of residing somewhere, to actually *be* there. Going home will be harder to adjust to, but that too will come to pass as you recall the parts of everyday life you enjoy.

Artist's and writers colonies often have minimum stays of one month, but some, such as Yaddo, let you stay for only two weeks, the same basic time period as a residency in a national park. This makes it easier for parents of young children, or people with nine-to-five jobs at companies with bosses that don't even know that they write poetry. Colonies and residencies require you to plan ahead because the applications are due about six months prior to the earliest time you would be able to stay there. They do ask that you describe the project you wish to work on, but they won't hold you to that. Once you are at a colony, you can write whatever you wish. However, a residency at a university will require a public reading from the work-in-progress. Since you are applying to get away from work and a month of mowing the lawn, however, it is quite possible that you will have had no time to work on the book project you detailed to the colony admissions and can get to work on it when you arrive.

When you choose the right environment for your temperament and writing, you can pack light and right, and wave good-bye to the life you lead for a brief sojourn at a colony or residence, get the most out of the experience, and make it last when you return.

AIR, a particularly apt acronym for the artist-in-residence programs in the national parks, currently accepts writers at nineteen of the thirty parks, and, in a marvel of abstraction, each AIR program is run by the park's Division of Interpretation. Glacier National Park only recently added writers to the list of possible interpreters of their landscape—and, as of this writing, has not yet accepted any. All of the programs offer less than ten residencies a year, and each applicant is in potential competition with artists of many disciplines, except at Devils Tower, which solely accepts writers.

Residencies occur one at a time, from one week to six in the milder months of a region. You might stay in a cabin, at a campground, or in an efficiency apartment, and you are free to roam. You must have a car and buy your own food, be in good health, and share a deep respect for the land. Some programs allow for loved ones to accompany you but not your pets, which are misinterpreted as unnatural predators and unlucky prey—a fierce reproach and exotic lure.

Some parks make you a volunteer and give you workers' compensation, in case, for example, you're bitten by one of the thirty varieties of rattlesnakes in the Mojave Desert. As with any residency, you must give back. In the National Parks, participants give a talk to interested staff and visitors, and donate a piece of writing from the residency. Choose carefully, since the park service will hold copyright and the rights to reproduce it, and it will become part of their history, and yours with them. If this isn't your kind of trade-off, apply to a colony instead—or to Devils Tower National Park, which asks only for you to contribute to their "Tower Story Box."

Writers who need more time than a week or two to devote to their books and who may benefit from research libraries should consider academic residencies in either a prep school or a university. These require the residents to interact with students, usually by teaching a class and giving a reading from a work-in-progress. There are writer-in-residence programs at many universities that invite accomplished writers to stay, but the ones in this book are for writers who have not yet published a first book or are between their first and second books. Some want applicants with an MFA, and some want only applicants who are outside of academia. But they all want the writers to be working on specific book projects.

The community-based AIR programs that do not invite writers or ask them to pay for their stay usually team up with local elementary schools or present their own programming that engages the public so that all a resident must do to give back is give a talk, teach a workshop, or give a presentation. A Studio in the Woods in New Orleans expects its residents to come to dinners with invited area artists, dancers, and writers, which doesn't seem like much of a hardship.

The following lists are selections from the larger list that is included on the attached CD-ROM, and it by no means indicates my preferences. (To include all in the book would have meant that you could use *An Insider's Guide to Creative Writing Programs* as a doorstop.) I chose some of the most well known here and abroad as well as some that are unusual or particularly spectacular. I urge you to go to these glorious websites, which will make you wonder why you've been sitting at your desk, writing at home.

Artist Colonies

Edward F. Albee Foundation
Montauk, New York

Five residents at a time stay for one month, June through September. The program is for writers, dancers, painters, sculptors, and composers. Applications can be submitted January 1 to April 1, and residents are notified by May 15.

"Bellagio's dreamlike locale, where glancing out the French windows into Lake Como, surrounded by the Alps and fronted by Italian villas, is mesmerizing. One faces a beautiful wall instead. Conversations with experts from all fields and countries—not just academic—enrich and inspire. I dined with a man who designed airports several times, causing me to re-think part of a poem that touched on weightlessness and design. Best of all, the staff makes all the visitors feel their privilege. There's even a button for summoning them!"

—Terese Svoboda, author of *Tin God* (University of Nebraska Press, 2006)

■ Who's Afraid of a Room of One's Own?

Two miles from the center of Montauk, a lighthouse town on the coast of Long Island on the Atlantic Ocean, is The William Flanagan Memorial Creative Persons Center. Known colloquially as "The Barn," it is tucked away in a knoll, and managed by the Edward F. Albee Foundation for the summertime use of talented writers, dancers, artists, and composers who require an undisturbed, peaceful environment in which to create. Albee, the anti-peachy-keen playwright, established the foundation in 1967 after his acclaimed, Tony Award–winning play "Who's Afraid of Virginia Woolf?" brought him plentiful proceeds.

The Barn is where the five residents live and work, and where they gather to cook meals from the food they purchase. It is simple communal housing with unmatched old furniture and an outdoor beach shower. You will need transportation—at least a bicycle, preferably a car.

You should request which month you want to stay and also list two alternate residency periods, and also mention if you are applying for residency elsewhere. Send twelve poems, one short story or two chapters of a novel, a play or screenplay manuscript, a résumé, two letters of recommendation, and a letter of intent.

Edward F. Albee Foundation, 14 Harrison St., New York, NY 10013, 212-226-2020, www.albeefoundation.org

Bellagio Study and Conference Center
Bellagio, Italy

Fifteen residents at one time, 140 per year, February to mid-December, minus June and July. Residencies are two weeks, three weeks, or thirty days. Application deadlines are well in advance of stay: early January for February to May of the following year; May 10 for April to May of the following year; and August 1 for August to mid-December of the following year.

■ Pearls of Wisdom

Pliny the Elder, that imaginative Roman whose thirty-seven-volume *Natural History* came out in 77 A.D., resided in Bellagio, "the pearl of the lake," where these days writers, scholars, artists, scientists, policy makers, and practitioners worldwide come to finish their latest projects with the generous support of The Rockefeller Foundation. Virgil considered Lake Como to be the greatest lake in Italy, and its pearl is considered one of the prettiest towns in Europe, and still work gets done by individuals, conferences, and teams at Bellagio Study and Conference Center.

It's a fifty-acre setting with parks, gardens, and historic buildings on the edge of Lake Como in the foothills of the Italian Alps, a two-hour drive from the Swiss border and an hour drive from Milan. Residents are housed in two buildings, the Maranese and Villa Serbolleni, in private rooms with baths, and a study adjoining or elsewhere on the grounds. A small library contains reference books, free access to the Internet, and the works of many former residents.

The globally conscious Rockefeller Foundation established Bellagio Study and Conference Center in 1959 to encourage freedom of thought, the privacy to create, and lively exchange. The Foundation's goals need not be reflected in the creative works of the applicants to Bellagio, however, just a certain accomplishment in their careers, excellence in writing, and the potential of proposed projects. Recent writers include Meena Alexander, Alfred Corn, Nicholas Delbanco, Galway Kinnell, Herbert Leibowitz, Dael Orlandersmith, Terese Svoboda, and Cecelia Vicuña.

A geographical diversity in the applicants' homelands is sought, as is ability to contribute to the intellectual mix of individuals from all around the world, including developing countries. One can reside only twice, no less than ten years apart, and applicants who have been rejected must wait two years before applying again. Spouses and other life partners are encouraged to accompany the resident or, if they are in one of the disciplines, may apply concurrently. Collaborative residencies are also accepted. Send a cover sheet, list of publications, and curriculum vitae with your detailed project description and three published reviews of your previous work. Decisions arrive four months after deadlines.

Room and board is part of the residency, but individuals must pay for phone, fax, and other personal expenses, as well as airfare to Milan. Assistance with round-trip economy airfare is largely available to applicants in developing countries and rarely to those in high-income countries.

Bellagio Center Office, The Rockefeller Foundation, 420 Fifth Ave., New York, NY 10018-2702, www.rockfound.org

Blue Mountain Center
Blue Mountain Lake, New York

The center offers fourteen four-week residencies at a time for creative and nonfiction writers, artists, activists, and musicians, usually June 15 to October 31. The application deadline is February 1. The center also offers the $5,000 Richard J. Margolis Award, which includes a residency; the deadline to apply is July 1.

■ Wild Blue Yonder

Blue Mountain Lake is a town in the southern Adirondack mountains, located in a park so huge it covers one third of New York State and competes with Alaska as one of the largest wildlife refuges in the country. In the pristine woods beside the Blue Mountain Lake is a quiet, ever-changing working community of socially conscious writers, artists, musicians, and activists thinking beyond the boundaries of culture.

The Adirondack Lodge that houses writers in pine bedrooms with studies and serves breakfast and dinner to them at a big table in the warm dining room dates back to the turn of the last century. Linens are provided, as well as laundry facilities, and there are hiking trails, a tennis court, and boats on the grounds. The odious telephone is coin-operated for your protection from the outside world, and messages can be taken in the office during the day. Recent writers include Celia Bland, Joe Connelly, Janice Eidus, Elizabeth Gaffney, Sybil Koller, Lisa Lerner, Vestal McIntyre, Sigrid Nunez, Richard Peabody, Hannah Tinti, and Gary Whitehead.

Send a brief biographical sketch including professional achievements; a statement of your plan for work; how you heard about BMC, including names of previous residents whom you know, if any; an unsigned sample, a maximum of thirty pages, double-spaced; your preference for dates (session 1: June 24 to July 22, session 2: July 29 to August 26, session 3: September 4 to October 2, session 4: October 7 to November 4); and a $20 application processing fee. Applications should be sent to the Admissions Committee at the address below. Decisions are made by March 31.

The Margolis Award, named after journalist and poet Richard J. Margolis, is given each year to a promising new essayist or journalist whose work combines warmth, humor, wisdom, and concern with social justice. Send at least two examples of your work (published or unpublished, thirty pages maximum) and a short biographical note including a description of the current and anticipated work. There must be three copies of these writing samples, and none will be returned. The winner is notified in November.

Blue Mountain Center, P.O. Box 109, Blue Mountain Lake, New York, NY 12812, 518-325-7391, www.bluemountaincenter.org, bmc@bluemountaincenter.org.

The Richard J. Margolis Award of the Blue Mountain Center, c/o Margolis & Associates, 137 Newbury Street, Second Floor, Boston, MA 02116

Camargo Foundation
Cassis, France

Approximately seven residents per fall or winter/spring semester for an average stay of four months. The application deadline is January 15.

■ **Thistle, Cistus, Rosemary, and Thyme**
Cassis is part of Provence in the south of France, where sow thistle, sage-leaved cistus, and the savory herbs rosemary and thyme are

grown—not to mention forests of the conical Pin d'Alep and scrubby kermes oak. Cassis history encompasses the young Napoléon Bonaparte mounting a cannon on a cliff, and Nazi occupation ruining the seascape with shipwrecks. Imagine for a moment the breathtaking beauty of Cap Canaille and the Mediterranean in warm, dry sunshine for four months, herb gardens, and trips into Aix Marseilles, and you'll easily see why the American painter, musician, and filmmaker Jerome Hill bought an estate there in 1939.

Hill's fortune came to him by way of his grandfather's work on the Great Northern Railroad, and his love of arts was instilled by his father, an amateur painter and art collector in Saint Paul, Minnesota. In 1967, Hill established the Camargo Foundation to allow for scholars, writers, visual artists, video artists, composers, media artists, photographers, and filmmakers to live in Cassis and work on specific projects.

Each resident receives a stipend of $3,500 and lives for a semester in a centrally heated, furnished apartment with views of the sea. Clean bed linens and towels, and the periodic cleaning of apartments are included in the residents' stay, and a washer and dryer are available at reasonable cost. Apartments do not have telephones, but residents may each borrow a mobile phone with thirty minutes of outgoing time and free unlimited incoming calls included. E-mail access is free but must be accessed on each resident's own modem. Among the other buildings are a library, music conference room, reading room, dark room, artist's studio, and music composition studio.

Once a week, residents come together to hear about one of the projects, and every semester there are events such as chamber music, poetry readings, film screenings, and day excursions. Aix Marseilles is a culturally rich area, and a mini-van will take people to town. Only spouses, life partners, and dependent minors who have been approved early on may visit, and no pets are allowed. There's no French language requirement, but if you stay four months in another country, it would behoove you to learn its language.

Recent writers include Nancy P. Arbuthnot, Jim Barnes, Henri Cole, Cusi Cram, Angie Cruz, Richard Foerster, Lynn Freed, Patricia Hampl, Laird Hunt, and Karen Volkman.

To apply, you must send an original set and five copies of the signed application form, a 1,000-word project proposal, curriculum vitae, three letters of recommendation, and up to thirty pages of current work. Creative writing samples will not be returned. Application forms are downloadable off the website, or can be sent by mail.

Ms. Ellen Guettler, Camargo Foundation, 125 Park Square Court, 400 Sibley St., Saint Paul, MN 55101-1928, www.camargofoundation.org

Château de La Napoule
La Napoule, France

Ten residents of different nationalities per six-week session for writers, musicians, dancers, designers, filmmakers, visual and performing artists. Application deadlines are August 1 for fall session and October 1 for winter/spring session.

■ By the Sea, the Beautiful Sea
Ahh, a castle on the Côte d'Azur, with a strange sculpture garden created by the late Henry and Marie Clews after they redecorated the place in funky neo-French medieval style. It was erected by the Villaneuve family in the fourteenth century and then destroyed and rebuilt, stubbornly, numerous times until the Clews bought the latest ruin in

1918. There are Roman and Saracen towers, terraces, a gatehouse, cloisters, a tea room, and four acres of walled, formal gardens— except for Mr. Clews's chubby stone birds and elongated figures— where treasure hunts for children frequently unfold. The Mediterranean Sea is right outside the castle, and Cannes is nearby.

The Clewses had a lifelong commitment to the Arts, and Château de La Napoule is a not-for-profit organization founded by Marie in 1956, and specializing in international multidisciplinary programs as an avenue for cultural exchange. Writers include Angie Cruz, Eric Gamalinda, Melissa Kirsch, Raimundo Mundo, Camilla Wood, and Harriet Zinnes.

This residency is for artists of national or international distinction, with well-established reputations, for whom a change of scenery might offer fresh inspiration, *and* for emerging artists with a record of solid achievement and potential, for whom an appointment as a resident artist might contribute to professional advancement. Send examples of your written work: poetry (a book or eight to ten poems), fiction (published work or a chapter of a manuscript), play (one complete script), stories or essays (two or three examples), nonfiction (a book or a selection from a manuscript).

Art Residencies, La Napoule Art Foundation, Château de La Napoule, 1, Avenue Henry Clews, 06210 Mandelieu—La Napoule, France, www.chateau-lanapoule.com

---

"Not only are you there to work but you are at the beach, down to the exquisite outdoor shower. Everyone is responsible for their own food and cooking. However, the communal living encourages shared meals and outings. My group of artists became a bit competitive and religious about cocktails, dinners, and grilling. We shared everything, but our personalities worked extremely well together, and we may have been an exception. One of the highlights of my time at The Barn was the mail delivery, which came in the gracious hands of Mr. Albee. This simple action was a very special honor for us all and oddly pushed you to work harder—perhaps even dream of being able to sponsor developing artists yourself someday."

—K. Kamal Ayyildiz, author of *The Cistern*
and former fellow at The Edward F. Albee Foundation

Chateau de Lavigny International Writer's Colony
Lausanne, Switzerland

Eight residents per three-week stay for writers of fiction, poetry, creative nonfiction, translation, plays, and screenplays from the beginning of June to mid-September. The application deadline is March 21.

■ Geneva Treat
Farm paths, a rose garden, terraces, green fields, vineyards, and Lake Geneva entreat writers to share their voices and create new work. Located in a small town between Geneva and Lausanne, the château looks out over the lake and the Alps. Resident writers give one evening reading per session in the Faulkner Room. They have private rooms and all of their meals are cooked for them. Common areas of the Château, as well as the gardens, are shared, and apart from occasional readings and exchanges with local literary guests, residents are left on their own to write in peace and beauty.

Founded by the late Jane Rowohlt in memory of her husband, the

German publisher Heinrich Maria Ledig-Rowohlt, whose name is also attached to Art Omi's Ledig House in Omi, New York, the Château de Lavigny offers and fosters "a spirit of international community and creativity." In 1996, a small, dedicated international committee of writers and administrators agreed to serve as volunteers to create this institution. While Ledig-Rowohlt published Albert Camus, William Faulkner, Ernest Hemingway, Günther Grass, Vladimir Nabokov, John Updike, Harold Pinter, Jean-Paul Sartre, and many other key twentieth-century writers, he always looked for new voices. In that spirit, the Château de Lavigney encourages emerging as well as established writers to apply. It looks for writers interested in exchanging their ideas as well as concentrating on their own work. Participating writers have included Scott Ely, Alvin Greenberg, Janet Holmes, Susan Ludvigson, Beryl Schlossman, Michael Waters, and Xu Xi.

Send a completed official application form with personal data and your first, second, and third choices of dates to stay; a short personal statement; a short statement about the project you will work on at Lavigny; a curriculum vitae of one page, including relevant publications and achievements; two independently posted letters of recommendation from published writers, critics, publishers, or translators; and a sample of your work, no more than eight pages. Applicants must have at least one book published (but not self-published), and be fluent in either English or French. They currently receive more than seventy applications from around the world each year. Acceptances are announced in April.

Fondation Ledig-Rowohlt, Montbenon 2, Case postale 5475, 1002
Lausanne, Switzerland, Chlavigny@hotmail.com,
www.chateaudelavigny.ch

Cove Park
Cove, Scotland

Seven residents at a time attend—writers of poetry, fiction, and criticism; environmental and visual artists; dancers and choreographers; theater directors; opera composers; actors; curators; and architects—May through the end of October. They hope to increase the number to ten artists and year-round residencies. Some residents have been invited and some have applied. Inquire about specific deadlines and opportunities.

■ Pod People
This cool place is a conservation park and an international artist colony in verdant western Scotland on the border of the Trossachs National Park. Grass-roof domed structures (pods) or converted freight cars (cubes) house the residents on the hillsides or the lip of Loch Long. A bridge designed by Richard La Trobe Bateman while in residence in 2001 connects the pods and cubes to the three-thousand-square-foot center where residents eat, rehearse, meet, read in the library, or participate in programs. Wild orchids, doves, highland cattle, sheep, and ducks thrive on the fifty-acre former farmland of Rosneath Peninsula, which is about an hour from Glasgow.

The pods are made of green oak and were purchased from a BBC program, Castaway, in the Hebrides, and upgraded by the original architect, Andy McAvoy, to incorporate both living and working spaces. The cubes were freight containers joined together by Urban Space Management, ironically, to create individual living spaces filled with light and covered in heather.

Eileen and Peter Jacobs founded Cove Park in 2000, a year after purchasing the park. Eileen is a Glaswegian occupational therapist and sculptor, and Peter is a mechanical engineer from Aylshire. It was Eileen's idea to create an artists residency center somewhere in the United Kingdom that would give individuals the time, space, and freedom to research and develop their ideas. Cove Park hosts conference groups and individuals at other times of the year, and during the artist residencies, supports and promotes the artists, creating opportunities through public participation in a related events program, as well as with website links to participating artists. Recent writers have included Chinese poet Yian Lang, Scottish poet and translator Harvey Holton, and Hungarian playwright András Forgách.

Send a curriculum vitae, artist's statement, and examples of your writing to be considered for the Scottish Arts Council International Literary Fellowship and Creative Writing Residencies. Be sure to include the right sized SASE.

The nearest international airport, one hour away, is in Glasgow, and trains leave from London and Glasgow.

Alexia Holt, Director, Cove Park, Peaton Hill, Cove, Argyll and Bute, Scotland G84 0PE, 01436-860123, information@covepark.org, www.covepark.org

Hall Farm Center for Arts & Education
Townshend, Vermont

Four to five residencies at a time, lasting one to six weeks June through September, for writers and artists at all levels. The application deadline is February 1. List format in April.

■ **School's Out**

Work, relax, reflect, and be inspired by the rolling pastures, woods, and cool pond. The two-hundred-year-old farm, which combines the life of quiet contemplation and the creative process, was founded in 1999 by public school teachers Scott Browning and Phillip School-man. They lamented the erosion of the role of arts in the classroom, and the marginalization of the arts and artist in society. Since it is commonly understood that the arts are an unparalleled tool in childhood development, Browning and Schoolman provide the resources for the integration of arts in education by supporting teachers who are committed to bringing art into the classroom, fostering collaborations with public schools, colleges, and teacher-training institutes, and by nurturing the creative process of emerging and established artists.

Renovated with the spirit of the 1800s, the house nonetheless has electricity and phone service. Writers can stay upstairs in the bedroom studios or separately at the pond house. The barn houses the library. Breakfast, lunch, and snacks are self-serve, and dinner is prepared by the resident chef.

Writers include Lisa Lerner, James Najarian, Penny Wolfsen, Carol Zoref.

Send a completed application form with résumé, project statement, writing sample, and space requirements. The writing sample should be two copies of no more than thirty pages, printed on single sides and double-spaced for nonfiction, drama, fiction, and poetry.

Hall Farm Center for Arts & Education, 392 Hall Drive, Townshend, VT 05353, 802-365-4483, info@hallfarm.org, www.hallfarm.org

Hawthornden Castle International Retreat for Writers
Midlothian, Scotland

Five one-month residencies for writers at one time. The application deadline is the end of September for the following year.

■ A Poet's Home Is His Castle

Located a mile east of Roslin, and situated on the lush banks of River North Esk, the pretty Hawthornden looks more like a large stone house with a few fairytale features. And in fact it was the home of the poet William Drummond, who built a house around the ruined tower in 1638. And while Ben Johnson and Samuel Johnson came to stay, the real history is held in the caves below that once sheltered Robert the Bruce. The Drummond family held on to it until 1970, and then in 1982, it became the International Writers Retreat, keeping it in the literary family.

Send for the application packet. They prefer published authors. Writers include Helen Vendler, Sharon Mesmer, Michael Lowenthal, and Bertha Rogers.

Hawthornden Castle, The International Retreat for Writers, Lasswade, Midlothian EH18 1EG, 0131 440 2180

Hedgebrook: A Retreat for Women Writers
Whidbey Island, Washington

Fifty-six residencies are available from March to mid-November, for two weeks to two months. Six writers are in residence at a time. Special diets are accommodated, as are writers who are vision or hearing impaired. Hedgebrook is not wheelchair accessible. Application deadlines are October 1 for March to May 31, and March 15 for June to Thanksgiving.

■ Good for Knitting, Bad for Allergies

Even if the forty-eight-acre Hedgebrook does not engage the island's new, silky-soft lawn mowers in their organic land-management plan, applicants with wool allergies should stock their medicine bags. "Whidbey Island is lousy with llamas and alpacas," a former islander reports. An oasis on the south end of bucolic Whidbey, thirty-five miles northwest of Seattle, Hedgebrook overlooks Puget Sound. On clear days, Mount Rainier is visible in the distance. Intended as an inspiring environment for creativity, there are mature, second-growth fir and cedar forests, meadows, brooks, ponds, waterfalls, a goddess garden, and two organic vegetable gardens. South Whidbey weather is mild, from the 50s to the mid 70s, with highest rainfall (one to two inches) in the spring and fall.

This colony has six beautifully designed studio buildings, each made of a different type of wood, with indoor color schemes, pottery sinks, and stained glass windows. The farmhouse is the social building with library, living room, and dining area. Organic produce from the garden is prepared by one of three chefs and distributed in lunch baskets or on dishes in the dining room overlooking Deer Lagoon.

Since Hedgebrook opened in 1988, it has supported eight hundred women writers of diverse cultural backgrounds and a wide range of ages from around the world, including Barbados, Canada, England, South Africa, the Philippines, Thailand, Zimbabwe, and the United States. The board of directors of this not-for-profit colony are also culturally diverse and involved in social, political, and environmental issues and organizations. The staff began a land-management plan of organic farming in 1998 that charts how the retreat land is tended and managed, to demonstrate to the larger community that organic farming and natural land management is viable. Hedgebrook hosts other events, including the "Women Playwrights Festival" and "Poetry By the Ponds." Recent writers are Monique Truong, Jacqueline Woodson, and Sandra Seaton.

A diverse cultural and literary community of women writers is encouraged. Writers at various stages of their careers are welcome, regardless of publication history. But you can reside at beautiful Hedgebrook only once—no repeat stays.

There are fellowships and travel stipends available, so do inquire. Otherwise, you must pay for your flight, train, or bus ticket to Seattle, and the ferry to the island, where a staff member will meet you. There is also an application fee of $15.

Hedgebrook: A Retreat for Women Writers, 2197 Millman Road, Langley, WA 98260, Hedgebrk@whidbey.com, www.hedgebrook.org

---

"I chose Jentel because they are small and I like the adventure of intimacy with people I haven't selected; and the spaciousness of Wyoming appealed to me; and they had a simple, clean website. The preponderance of visual artists there is also attractive: it's interesting to sense the working ways of other creative forms, and to sense that from a minority place. I simply applied, following their guidelines. Jentel is encouraging collaborative projects, which fit for a friend and I who had been independently working on the same subject, and wanted to explore multimedia avenues."

—Carolyn Dille, poet

Jentel Artist Residency Program
Banner, Wyoming

The program offers five residencies at a time almost year-round for artists and writers. Application deadlines are Sept 15 for residencies from January 15 to May 13, and January 15 for residencies from May 15 to December 13.

■ A Thousand Acres
In the lower Piney Creek Valley beside the majestic Bighorn Mountains, a thousand acres of hay and alfalfa feed the cattle ranch. This is big sky country, with sage-scented hills and five little studio buildings for artists and writers to get away from the madding crowd. An old log cabin serves as headquarters on this working cattle ranch. Each resident is offered separate living accommodations and a workspace. Large, well-lit studios are equipped with running water and adequate light for late work. Writers need to bring typewriters or laptops. Common areas include a library, kitchen, great room, and recreation area. A monthly stipend is provided to defray personal expenses.

The Jentel Foundation, founded by Neltje, a Wyoming painter who is heir to Doubleday publishing, strives to protect and sustain the pristine natural environment of the Piney Creek Valley by protecting and responsibly managing the unique plants and wildlife, by preserving the land from development, by protecting and preserving the Indian artifacts, by protecting and preserving any geological phenomena, and through responsible land-management practices. The residency program provides time and space away from everyday normal life to create substantive work in an unfettered environment. There's an airport in Sheridan, twenty miles away, with connections to Denver International Airport.

Send a completed application form, two letters of reference, and two copies of a ten- to twenty-page writing sample with an SASE.

Jentel Artist Residency Program, 130 Lower Piney Creek Road, Banner, WY 82832, www.jentelarts.org

Ledig House International Writers' Residency
Omi, New York

Forty to fifty residents each year in writing, art, dance, and music, and ten writing residents at a time for one week to two months in the spring session, April 1 to June 24, or the fall session, August 24 to October 31. The application deadline is November 30.

■ Outstanding In Their Fields

Ledig House is situated on a hill above "The Fields" modern sculpture garden in view of the Catskill Mountains in the Hudson River Valley. The three hundred acres of Art Omi International Art Center is two and a half hours from New York City. Named after Heinrich Maria Ledig-Rowohlt, a German publisher who chose an outstanding range of authors, from William Faulkner to Thomas Pynchon, Jean-Paul Sartre to Toni Morrison. A jubilant Faulkner signing his book to Ledig-Rowohlt is one of many photographs in the house.

The rooms have an almost Shaker simplicity to them, with a bed, a desk, and a beautiful view. Ledig House provides all meals, and each night a cook prepares dinner. Days are reserved as quiet hours, while evenings afford a more communal environment. During each session, several guests from the New York publishing community are invited for dinner and discussion. Bicycles, a swimming pool, and a nearby tennis court are available.

Art Omi believes that creative work is a vehicle for knowledge and understanding that transcends political and cultural boundaries, and to this end has hosted more than four hundred residents from fifty different countries to date. Other International Residencies are given in dance, music, and art. Recent fellows include Amy Benson, Agymah Kamau, Sarah Manguso, Wyatt Mason, and Timothy Sergay.

Send a biographical sketch, including publications, performances, and writing credits; one nonreturnable copy of your latest published work, or, if unpublished, a ten-page sample of your latest work; a one-page description of the work to be undertaken while at Ledig House; a letter of recommendation; a self-addressed envelope for notification; and a telephone number or e-mail address where you can be reached. The Geraldine R. Dodge Foundation Fellowship for a New Jersey Writer is awarded yearly to a resident New Jersey writer for two months at Ledig House. To apply for this scholarship, add "New Jersey Writers Fellowship" to the address for applications.

Ledig House Applications, 55 Fifth Ave., 15th floor, New York, NY 10003, 212-206-6114, artomi55@aol.com, www.artomi.org/ao/ledig.htm

The Leguria Study Center
Bogliasco, Italy

Sixteen four- to six-week residencies at one time, September 11 to December 15 and February 12 to May 18, for people doing creative and scholarly work. The application deadline is January 15 for fall and winter, April 15 for winter and spring.

■ Tangerine Dreams

Bogliasco is a maritime village with pink and cream houses, a pebbly beach, a single-span medieval bridge built on Roman ruins, and inlets and high cliffs and walls that conceal exotic gardens of cypress, cactus, and groves of tangerine. The Leguria Study Center is comprised of three separate properties. Villa dei Pini follows the traces of an ancient Roman road through pines and a garden to a sharp drop to the rocky seashore. Villa Orbiana and Villa Rincon are further up the Apennines in an olive grove, a five-minute walk from Villa dei Pini. Each of the villas contains private living quarters, studios equipped with computers, and common rooms. Everywhere are the spectacular views of the Mediterranean Sea and the Ligurian coastline to inspire. The Russian composer Alexander Skryabin benefited from the calm there. After leaving his wife in 1905 and running off with his mistress, Tatyana Schloezer, he completed a large portion of "Ecstasy Poem," one of his major works.

Send the completed application form with your preferences for residency dates; a short-form curriculum vitae, no more than three pages; a one-page description of the project you intend to work on; three reference letters; and a sample of the applicant's work, submitted in triplicate.

Bogliasco is situated on the southeastern city limits of Genoa on the Italian Riviera in the north. Genoa is the capital of the Liguria region, a university town, and one of the most important cities in Italy. The Genoa international airport, a thirty-minute automobile ride from the Study Center, currently has daily connections to and from Frankfurt, London, Milan, Munich, Rome, and Paris.

The Bogliasco Foundation, 885 Second Ave., New York, NY 10017-2299, 212-940-8204, info@bfny.org, www.leguriacenter.org

MacDowell Colony
Peterborough, New Hampshire

Twenty to thirty residents at a time for one to two months January through November for writers, artists, musicians, architects, landscapers, film/video arts, translators, and interdisciplinary artists. Application deadlines are September 15 for February through May residencies, January 15 for June through September, and April 15 for October through January. These are not postmark deadlines, so send your application well before those dates.

■ Smooth Living

The Abenaki Indians called the 3,165-foot mountain Monadnock because it was smooth, and composer Edward MacDowell claimed he wrote smoother music at his summer farm in Peterborough. A founder of The Academy in Rome, MacDowell knew well the benefit of artists of different disciplines working together, so he and his wife, Marion, set about creating an artists colony on the land. Blue herons, bald eagles, and moon loons reside in the area, and three protected rivers run through Peterborough. The MacDowells had friends in high places—Grover Cleveland, Andrew Carnegie, and J. P. Morgan—who set up a fund, and Edward lived long enough for the first colonists to arrive in 1907. Marion held on until 1956, touring the country and giving lectures and raising money for the fund. When they were not famous, Studs Terkel, Oscar Hijuelos, Thornton Wilder, Alice Walker, Willa Cather, and James Baldwin all came to stay.

As the first artists colony in the United States, MacDowell Colony established a set of rules that the others have adapted. There is a balance of social interaction and focus on work, and no one is to visit any other artist without permission. Lunch is delivered to the private studio, and breakfast and dinner are served in the dining room. Informal gatherings can occur.

Spread out over the four hundred fifty acres of woodland and fields, MacDowell studios have names like Mansfield, Alexander, Mixter, Monday Music, Firth, New Jersey, and Star. They are tiny houses made of stone or wood with shutters, screen porches, and verandas, or modern structures with large windows, or tropical cabins on stilts. Each has privacy to the extent of not being in view of its neighbor.

Submit the two-page application form, six copies of a work sample, a project description, two references, and a $20 fee. The writing sample should be six to ten poems, two to three short stories or chapters, or twenty to thirty pages, two to three essays or articles, a complete play script, or a complete or excerpted libretto score and audio recording. Acceptance or rejection comes two months after the deadline.

Recent residents include Benjamin Anastas, Donald Antrim, April Bernard, Star Black, Michael Chabon, Lan Samantha Chang, Carolyn Chute, Stephen Dunn, Cathy Park Hong, Christine Hume, Lewis Hyde, Agymah Kamau, Marilyn Krysl, Margot Livesy, Barry Lopez, Alessandra Lynch, Sarrah Mangold, Nicholas Montemorano, Chris Offutt, Wendy Salinger, Ravi Shankar, Charlie Smith, Lynn Tillman, Genya Turovskaya, Wendy Wasserstein, Susan Yankowitz.

Admissions Coordinator, MacDowell Colony, 100 High St., Peterborough, NH 03458, 603-924-3886, 212-966-4860, admissions@macdowellcolony.org

Millay Colony
Austerlitz, New York

Six one-month residencies at a time for writers, visual artists, composers, filmmakers, and video artists April through November. The application deadline is October 1.

■ Burning the Candle at Both Ends?

Steepletop is six hundred thirty-five acres of land, one third owned by The Millay Colony and two thirds by the Edna St. Vincent Millay Society, which manages the estate and gardens. Steepletop Barn was built in the 1920s by "Vincent," as Millay was known, and later renovated by the colony to provide studios and bedrooms for four residents. The first American poet to win a Pulitzer Prize, Edna St. Vincent Millay (1892–1950)—whose most famous poem, "First Fig," reads, "My candle burns at both ends;/It will not last the night;/But ah, my foes, and oh, my friends—/It gives a lovely light!"—died at her beautiful home in Austerlitz.

The main building was added in 1997 and comfortably accommodates artists with disabilities. It has a kitchen, dining/living area, music room/library, laundry, public bathroom, and phone room with Internet access. The Speinson Studio in this building has a studio with two rooms that works well for writers and artists who may need an aide to stay, or for any of the residents working in collaboration.

Residents get a private room and studio, prepare their own breakfasts, and have lunches and weekday meals provided by the colony. No social gatherings are required. Residents may walk to local stores, the bank, or the library. A state forest borders the land.

Send a completed application form, an artist statement of less than a page, a one- to two-page biographical statement, and three copies of either a) no more than thirty pages in manuscript form, or b) up to fifteen poems in manuscript form. There is a $30 application fee.

Writers have included Jennifer Barber, Judith Baumel, Madeline Beckman, Xam Carter, Jan Clausen, Cornelius Eady, Therese Eiben, Colette Inez, Ann Keniston, Susan Kwok Kim, Samuel Menashe, David Morse, Sigrid Nunez, Carl Phillips, Martha Rhodes, Prageeta Sharma, and Brian Swann.

Administrative Office, Millay Colony, P.O. Box 3, Austerlitz, NY 12017-0003, 518-392-3103, apply@millaycolony.org, www.millaycolony.org

---

"At Yaddo they may bring lunch in a pail, but at Hawthornden there's lunch plus, every afternoon, high tea, including home-baked goodies like 'millionaire shortbread' (worth the trip to Scotland!). Having the full run of a seventeenth-century castle, and being treated so royally by the staff, made me feel like writing was a bona fide—more than that: exalted—pursuit. I wrote the first chapter of a novel, took long walks through the glen, caught the bus into Edinburgh frequently—all this, and still plenty of time for getting to know the wonderfully international group of fellows: Dutch, Polish, British, and Canadian."

—Michael Lowenthal, author of *Avoidance* (Graywolf Press, 2002)
and *The Same Embrace* (Plume, 1999)

Sacatar Foundation
Bahia, Brazil

Fifteen to twenty-five residencies a year for six to twelve weeks for artists and writers.

■ Going Coconuts

Crescent-shaped Itaparica is the largest of fifty-six islands in the pale blue Bay of all Saints, across from the city of Salvador in Bahia, Brazil, where old VW buses serve as taxis. There is a mix of Brazilian and international artists at the vibrant Quinta Pitanga estate run by the Sacatar Foundation, which invites people to come hither by saying: "No previous knowledge of Bahia is required, but we seek applicants who have the flexibility and stamina to dance with the unknown." Speaking of which, Samba and the joyful Chula are the musical dances of Bahia, a multicultural mix of African, Portuguese, French, and native Indian. This is a tranquil estate in a carnival atmosphere, so be ready to join the party. Residents' rooms are furnished with double beds and have attached bathrooms. The estate is beset with coconut palms, green lawns, little courtyards, filigree ironwork, and ponds.

Send three printed copies of no more than thirty pages, comprising a short story, a one-act play, a portion of a novel or play, a portion of a screenplay, or an essay. Poets should send ten short poems or an appropriate excerpt from a longer piece. Seeing eye dogs are welcome, but pets are not. The wide halls and doorways accommodate writers with some disabilities and the writer's caretaker may be approved to come, but the rest of the island is not as accessible. The Sacatar Foundation pays for your international travel, but there is no stipend. You must pay for incidental expenses and local transportation on the island, but they are happy to come pick you up at the airport. Internet access is available at the Quinta Ranch, and in the town of Itaparica.

Admissions, Sacatar Foundation, P.O. Box 2612, Pasadena, CA 91102-2612, info@sacatar.org, www.sacatar.org

Wildacres
Little Switzerland, North Carolina

One-week residencies for writers, artists, and musicians May through October. The application deadline is February 15.

■ Birds of a Feather

Established as a foundation for the betterment of human relations, Wildacres is a far cry from the resort for actors and writers the original owner, Thomas Dixon, tried to create in the 1920s on one thousand acres in Pisgah National Forest of the Blue Ridge mountains before the 1929 stock market crash. Dixon was a preacher, lawyer, actor, playwright, novelist, and legislator whose novel *The Clansman* was made into the controversial and successful movie *The Birth of a Nation*. A Texas Bank got hold of the land first, and then Jinks Harrell, a real estate agent, nudged I. D. Blumenthal, founder of Radiator Specialty company, to buy the irresistible landscape for $6,500, even though it was listed at $190,000. Blumenthal drove the county clerk up the mountain to view the lot when a fog descended and obscured the view. They couldn't see their hands in front of their faces and Blumenthal led him through eerie boarded-up shelters until the man fled, proclaiming the place godforsaken, and Blumenthal got his deal. He believed the place should be used for interfaith gatherings. From spring through to autumn, writers can spend a week a quarter mile from the top of the retreat, in the rustic Owl's Nest Cabin, which looks like it is all roof, with deck and windows for eyes. Meals can be prepared in the kitchen of the Owl's Nest Cabin, or eaten at the Wildacres facilities at no charge.

Complete the application form with a description of yourself and project, and why you think a week at Wildacres would benefit you.

Wildacres, P.O. Box 280, Little Switzerland, NC 28749-0280, 828-756-4573, wildacres@wildacres.org, www.wildacres.org

Helene Wurlitzer Foundation
Taos, New Mexico

The foundation offers eleven three-month or more residencies at one time for writers of poetry, fiction, plays, and screenplays; artists; and composers April 1 through October 30. Applications are accepted throughout the year but must be received by January 31 for residencies the following year.

■ **Birds, Beasts, and Flowers**
Taos is a four-hundred-year-old settlement about an hour's drive north of Santa Fe in New Mexico's Sangre de Cristo Mountains. The Taos Pueblo dates back to 1000 A.D. and holds tours, but you'll be too busy doing nothing and writing in one of the eleven guest houses of the peaceful haven Helene Wurlitzer (who said, "Having to do something is guaranteed to destroy the creativity in anyone") set up in 1956 on eighteen acres of land. Since you'll be in residence for at least three months, take a drive into the mountains, past the Rio Grande, to visit D. H. Lawrence's tomb in a little open, round house with painted rose windows, overlooking northern New Mexico, and ponder the roadrunners, eagles, bears, snakes, poppies, and Indian paintbrush that inhabit and cling to Lawrence's world as well as yours.

The foundation keeps a low profile and grants rent- and utility-free housing during your stay. Three houses are designated for visual artists, three for composers, and six for literary artists. Each house, for single occupancy only, is independent from neighboring resident houses and fully furnished.

Send completed application, which includes a bio and résumé; a writing sample of one chapter and/or two short stories, not to exceed thirty pages, five or six poems, or one act of a play or screenplay; three references; and an SASE. Winners will be notified March 30.

Helene Wurlitzer Foundation, P.O. Box 1891, Taos, NM 87571, 505-758-2413, hwf@taosnet.com

Yaddo
Saratoga Springs, New York

Residencies are available year-round for two weeks to two months. The deadlines are January 15 for mid-May to February, and August 1 for late October through mid-May. Results are mailed April 1 and October 1.

■ I'll Spring You
Saratoga Springs is nestled in the southern foothills of the Adirondack Mountain range in northern New York State at an elevation of 1,400 feet. You will see it mentioned in both *Town & Country* and *American Turf Monthly*, a thoroughbred handicapping magazine, thanks to the nearby Saratoga Raceway that springs to life each August. But the real springs are mineral, first offered by the Algonquins to soldiers to heal rheumatism, neuralgia, intermittent fever, kidney and liver trouble, scrofulous diseases, and impurities of the blood. Spring comes late to the mountains, sometimes poking floral heads through blankets of snow in June.

Yaddo has four hundred acres of fields, hills, ponds, bridges, gardens, and woods for writers to unwind in before returning to their private bedrooms and studios in the stone mansion. All meals are provided to residents, breakfast and dinner in a dining hall and lunch pails left outside residents' rooms. It is said that author Katrina Trask, nee Kate Nichols of Brooklyn, saw into the future to a time when as yet unborn artists, composers, and writers would wander the mystical grounds of her estate, "creating, creating, creating." It was an adventurous and treacherous road to the "new, unique experiment" that would open in 1926, four years after Katrina's death. The acreage on which were built the many buildings and little island bridges was purchased in 1881 by Wall Street financier and photographer Spencer Trask. The pre-fire house was named Yaddo by their small daughter, who was thinking "shadow," and the Trasks entertained writers, politicians, industrialists, composers, and artists of their day in the beautiful Lake George community. It seemed an impossible dream when all four of the Trasks' children died in childhood and Spencer perished in a grisly train wreck. Katrina became reclusive and married family friend George Foster Peabody. Together they built up the trust that would support a working artist's community, and Peabody oversaw its completion after Katrina's death.

Most recently, the writing residents have included Chana Bloch, Anne Carson, Michael Harper, Maggie Estep, Sarah Arvio, Carl Bernstein, Jonathan Ames, Marilyn Chin, Star Black, and Xui Di.

Writers at all levels of their careers are encouraged to apply. A new panel of artists, composers, and writers review applications each period, and waiting lists are common.

Send the original and two copies of the completed application form, three copies of résumé and work samples (30 pages prose, 10 pages poetry), two letters of support, $20 application fee, and self-addressed postcard for notification of receipt. Parts of this application process can be completed online.

Yaddo, P.O. Box 395, Saratoga Springs, NY 12866, 518-548-0745, lleduc@yaddo.org, www.yaddo.org

---

"Camargo gave me a book I could never have written quite as I did without the dream of being there while I was working on it. And it gave me the south of France—which means two more books I'm working on now as a result of my experience, as well as friends I cherish from my residency. That's not just a gift but a form of enchantment I'll always be grateful for. I was tempted to barricade myself in my apartment and wait for the *pompiers* to come and haul me out. I always heard the rumor that Jerome Hill was uncommonly generous. Clearly, his spirit lives on."

—Patricia Hampl, author of *I Could Tell You Stories: Sojourns in the Land of Memory* (W. W. Norton, 2000)

Air Programs in the National Parks

Badlands National Park
Interior, South Dakota

RESIDENCY: 4 to 6 weeks March 15 to November 15 (excluding May 15 to September 7) for qualifying national and international writers, musicians, and visual artists.

APPLICATION DETAILS: Send a résumé and summary of creative works, artist's statement, up to three choices of beginning and ending dates, and a maximum of ten double-spaced pages of your writing. Selection panels convening in late January and early July make selections based on artistic integrity; ability to reside in a remote, rural area, willingness to donate a finished piece of work inspired by the stay; and ability to relate to school-age children. Deadlines are July 15 for fall and December 31 for spring.

RESIDENCY REQUIREMENTS: Residents must give a public education program and at least two talks or workshops to middle- or high-school students, and donate a piece of writing representative of residency and your style.

■ Martin Sheen and Sissy Spacek

Admit it: the 1973 Terrence Malick movie *Badlands* springs to mind, with the silken, young Martin Sheen and sparkling Sissy Spacek doing harm. Badlands National Park in southwestern South Dakota is even more memorable: a harsh 244,000 acres of sharp, windswept buttes, spires, pinnacles, and vast mixed prairies of blue grama, wheatgrass, green needle, buffalo, and needle-and-thread grasses, hiding an extraordinarily vital treasure of life with potential for regeneration. Here resides a record of eleven thousand years of human history, and thirty-five-million-year-old Oligocene fossil beds, while the black-footed ferret, the most endangered land mammal in North America (who knew?) is being reintroduced to the fifty-six varieties of grass. Paleontologists can come to trace the evolution of the horse, sheep, rhinoceros, and pig in these Badlands formations, which look like salt crystals on a tray in a childhood science project.

Writers are provided with an either fully furnished efficiency or one-bedroom apartment in a small housing complex near the park's entrance; access to the library, where there are computers with Windows installed; and use of bicycles. The apartments have basic cooking equipment and both heat and air-conditioning, which is a godsend in the weather extremes of blizzards and temperatures above 100 degrees Fahrenheit. Those who are selected for residency are entered into the volunteer program and covered under workers' compensation for any injuries incurred while in the park.

The Badlands was named a national monument in 1939 to preserve its fossil beds and "stunning geological scenery" and was redesignated a national park in 1978 to add to that the protection of its prairie ecosystem and anthropological history. Although French Canadian trappers and fur traders passed through The Badlands, the area is chiefly a hunting record of the Sioux, mixed with a gigantic fossil record. The Oglala Sioux comanage an area of the park called The Stronghold, where one of the last known Ghost Dances occurred in 1890 before the massacre at Wounded Knee, forty-five miles away.

The Badlands Natural History Association supports research and education at the Badlands National Park, and profits from sales are donated to the park to provide many services and to support the artist-in-residency program established in 1997. This AIR program is part of an international alliance of national parks and international nature reserves, including Rocky Mountain National Park in Estes Park, Colorado, and the Vashlovani Nature Reserve in Russia.

Consider the cost of travel and meals for the four- to six-week period, which may include airfare, train travel, fuel purchase, and the renting of a car; the Park Service will reimburse you for up to $300 in expenses. Bring bedding, personal gear, and writing supplies.

Artist-in-Residence Coordinator, Artist-in-Residence Program, Badlands NP, P.O. Box 6, Interior, South Dakota 57750, 605-433-5245, badl_information@nps.org, www.nps.gov/badl

Buffalo National River
Harrison, Arkansas

RESIDENCY: Three weeks in the spring (March to May), summer (June to August) and fall (September to November) for one individual a season in writing, art, music composition, and performance. It is not wheelchair accessible.

APPLICATION DETAILS: A panel of judges in all the artistic disciplines represented review the applications, and a large part of the selection is based on the writer's ability to interpret and integrate the park in the creation of work, willingness to volunteer, and artistic integrity. However, one must also submit a one- to two-page résumé and summary of works, a brief manuscript, an artist's statement, entry form, an SASE, and the desired time for residency. The deadline is January 31.

RESIDENCY REQUIREMENTS: Share the experience with park staff and visitors through a talk, lecture, or presentation of no more than a few hours. The resident will be enrolled in the National Park Service's Volunteers in Parks program. You must also donate a piece of writing representative of residency for the park to use in an appropriate way.

■ **Orange Is the New Black**
The nearly ninety-five-thousand acre Buffalo River National Park is not just one hundred thirty-five miles of unpolluted river through the Ozark Mountains, but also open farmlands, ponds, streams, historical and prehistoric sites, oak and hickory forests, lichen akin to that on the Arctic tundra, ferns, four-hundred-forty-foot dolomite and limestone bluffs, and box canyons. Armadillos, roadrunners, and scorpions live here, along with fifty-nine species of clearwater fish, white-tailed deer,

mink, bobcats, raccoons, and opossum. Since hunting is allowed in accordance with state regulations during most months of the year, writers should begin stocking up on the many styles of orange clothing available to them in the fashion world. There are a variety of hiking trips in the park, including a 2.1-mile journey into Lost Valley with cliffs, bluff shelters, a natural bridge, wildflowers, and a two-hundred-foot-long cave opening onto a waterfall. Some other trails take you back in time to Civilian Conservation Corps structures, the 1930s Collier Homestead at Tyler Bend, Rush Mining District, the Taylor Hickman Farmstead in Erbie, and more bluff shelters once occupied by paleo-Indians. Both bank and float fishing are enjoyed. Lodging is available in cabins in the park.

Coordinator, Artist-in-Residence Program, Buffalo National River, 402 N. Walnut, Suite 136, Harrison, AR 72601, 870-741-5443, buff_information@nps. gov, www.nps.gov/buff/artist2.htm

Devils Tower National Monument
Devils Tower, Wyoming

RESIDENCY: One week in September and October for two writers a year. Open to writers of essays, poetry, fiction, and nonfiction

APPLICATION DETAILS: One ten-page manuscript, twenty-five hundred words maximum, double-spaced for prose, single-spaced for poetry. Only U.S. citizens may apply. The deadline is April 1. Winners are announced May 15. Winning writers may reside again but may not reapply for five years.

RESIDENCY REQUIREMENT: Winners must contribute to the Tower Story Box and answer the question, "What Does the Tower Mean to You?" by application deadline of following year. This will be used in future exhibitions, publications, and programs.

■ Literature in the Making? Bear Right. Rite?

While my generation may know the igneous intrusion that rises out of a ponderosa pine forest from the wide eyes of Richard Dreyfus and Melinda Dillon in *Close Encounters of the Third Kind,* and rock climbers may revere Devils Tower as among the finest crack-climbing places in North America, twenty Plains Indian tribes, from Blackfeet to Rosebud Lakota, Pigeon to Flandreau Santee Dakota, Northern and Southern Arapaho, Crow and Cheyenne, consider climbing the sacred rock to be a desecration. Some of the tribal names for it translate to "Mythic-owl Mountain" (Lakota) or "Aloft on a Rock" (Kiowa), but most call it "Bear's Tipi," "Bear's Lodge," or "Bear's Lair" (Arapaho, Cheyenne, Crow). Out of respect for the people who have sun rituals, origin legends, vision quests, and rites centered on Bear's Tipi, The Devils Mountain National Monument management request that climbers refrain from edging their way up the hundreds of cracks—one four hundred feet—in the month of June, when most ceremonies occur; as a result, climbing that month has gone down 80 percent.

The park is alive with flower varieties that call out to the muses while satisfying the senses: False Solomon's Seal, field mint, Prairie Goldenpeas, blue-eyed grass, Evening Primrose, pussytoes, Miner's Candle, buttercups, Ten-petal Blazing Stars, Ball-headed Gilas, Virgin's Bower, sunflowers, Mountain waterparsnips, and wild licorice. Overhead and wading around are turkey vultures, doves, hairy woodpeckers, great blue herons, American kestrels, robins, red-tailed hawks, bats, and the rare green heron, American white pelican, and double-crested cormorant. Mix into this, at the very least, foxes, wolves, shrews, jackrabbits, minks, grizzlies, porcupines, badgers, beavers, northern leopard frogs, Eastern yellow-bellied racers, lynx, bison, snapping turtles, prairie dogs, and bighorn sheep.

Devils Tower National Monument aims to provide an inspiring, secluded working environment for promising writers. Modest lodging is available on park property in efficiency apartments, with back windows looking out onto the Tower. Writers drive to the park, which is in a remote northeastern part of the state, and purchase groceries to prepare themselves. Most writers stop at the supermarkets in the bigger towns on the way to park to start their residency. By residing in October, writers miss out on the severe thunder and lightning storms of summer and winter but can still expect rapid climactic changes and generally cool temperatures.

Theodore Roosevelt designated the 1,267-foot Devils Tower as our first National Monument on September 24, 1906. Devils Tower offers the only AIR program solely for writers, because they have partnered with Bearlodge Writers, a writers group with members in Wyoming and South Dakota. A quote on the website from the Pulitzer Prize–winning author N. Scott Momaday, who is a Kiowa tribe member, from his 1969 novel *The Way to Rainy Mountain* describes the powerful, eerie place, and ends with "There are things in nature that engender an awful quiet in the heart of man; Devils Tower is one of them." This hardly seems the invitation, but in 2004, the AIR program received thirty-two applications from writers in sixteen states. Resident writers include Connie Brown, Kathleen Heideman, Jennifer Johnson, and Shana Youngdale.

You may need to consider airfare to the area, and definitely costs to rent a car, and the purchase of food. It is not just writers from the West applying, since both 2004 winners were from Minneapolis/ Saint Paul. Writers coming from more populated areas should take note that the largest nearby airport, with four airlines, is in Rapid City, South Dakota, and the closest place to buy food is at a small grocery store ten miles away. The Devils Tower Natural History Association provides writers with a $100 travel stipend.

Christine Czazasty, Chief of Interpretation, Devils Tower National Monument, P.O. Box 10, Devils Tower, WY 82714, 307-467-5283 ext. 24, deto_interpretation@nps.gov, www.nps.gov/deto/writersprogram.htm

Everglades National Park
Homestead, Florida

RESIDENCY: Two to four weeks each for composers, visual artists, and writers of poetry, fiction, and creative nonfiction throughout the year

APPLICATION DETAILS: Send a completed application form, two letters of recommendation, a six-page-maximum writing sample, and four copies each of an artist's statement (or what the Everglades residency will do for the writer), a one- to two-page résumé, and a one-page "statement of intent" (or what the writer intends to do during those two weeks). The deadline is October 1. A panel of arts educators, artists, and curators review applications each year. Selections are made based on the merit of the work and how the candidate's work can advance the mission of the Everglades National Park and the growth of the writer's work.

RESIDENCY REQUIREMENTS: Volunteer a few hours to visit with park visitors and staff. Donate to the park for their collection one-time publication rights of a piece of a literary work in the writer's style and reflecting the writer's residency.

■ See Ya Later, Alligator; in a While Crocodile

There is a wonderful array of large wading birds, butterflies, woodland animals, sable seaside sparrows, orchids, bromeliads, grass, West Indian manatees, various Atlantic and green turtles, tree snails, and Garber's Spurge, but let's not forget the endangered Florida panther, summer mosquitoes, and the sensational, no-place-else-on-earth, co-existing alligators and crocodiles. Unwelcome guests such as paperbark, Brazilian pepper, pythons, boa constrictors, parrots, parakeets, blue and spotted tilapias, and wild hogs have desecrated the already fragile ecosystem.

Only the intrepid camp out for two weeks in this locale (tip: Choose a motor home over a tent), and campsites are available near Homestead and the Anhinga trail in Royal Palm, at the coastal Flamingo on Florida Bay, and Everglades City on the West Coast next to the Ten Thousand Islands. Most residents opt for the apartment or cottage, available after April in Flamingo, and year-round in Royal Palm or Shark Valley, which is near Big Cypress National Preserve.

Established in 1947, The Everglades is the only subtropical wilderness in North America, which means it has warm, wet summers and no significant frost. It stretches from the southern tip of the Florida peninsula and most of Florida Bay, enduring annual drought, flood, fire, sunshine, and torrential rain. Among the newest members of the AIR programs in the national parks, this one was started in 2001 by the abstract artist and social activist Donna Marxer, who was its first resident.

Residents buy their own food and bring their own writing materials and personal belongings. Writers must be in good health, self-sufficient, and be able to work closely with park staff and community. All lodging, whether indoors or out, should be left clean and neat.

Donna Marxer, Coordinator, AIRIE, Everglades National Park, 4000l State Road 9336, Homestead, FL 33034-6733, 305-242-7750, or 212-371-8733 for Donna Marxer, www.nps.gov/ever/current/airie.htm

---

"On Isle Royale, except for an hour a week talking to park visitors about nature writing, I was on my own to hike and canoe, and much of the writing I did was composed on the trail or the water, and later translated into frequent journal entries."

—Robert Root, nature writer

Glacier National Park
West Glacier, Montana

RESIDENCY: Four weeks in the summer for two national or international writers, painters, photographers, sculptors, filmmakers, composers, or musicians.

APPLICATION DETAILS: Send a one- to two-page résumé highlighting education, experience, and training, along with skills in presenting public education programs related to one's art, a publication summary, six to ten pages of writing about natural history or the cultural history of the area, a brief statement of intent, and a nonrefundable $10 application fee. Applications are updated in early to mid-fall of each year, so do check with the program for changes.

RESIDENCY REQUIREMENTS: Give three to five formal or informal educational presentations to the visiting public per week of residency, such as workshops, illustrated programs, demonstrations, or lessons. Donate a representative piece of writing to Glacier National Park for their collection.

■ Heaven Sent Me

Going-to-the-Sun Road wraps around the spectacular glaciated landscape of forests, alpine meadows, snow-streaked summits such as Heavens Peak, and lakes upon lakes. This is a million acres along the Great Divide with two hundred sixty species of birds and seventy species of mammals. The Great Northern Railroad was built through here, and buildings such as an old train depot and Lake MacDonald Lodge are protected. Now position yourself in a one-bedroom cottage on the shores of Lake MacDonald, with a sleeping loft that will accommodate three to four people. Your loved ones are welcome. Dispatch them to the seven hundred acres of hiking trails—you have writing to do.

Glacier became a National Park on May 11, 1910, but in 1932 Glacier and Waterton Lakes National Park, in Canada, were designated Waterton-Glacier International Peace Park. This designation celebrates the longstanding peace and friendship between the two nations. Glacier and Waterton Lakes have both been designated as Biosphere Reserves and together were recognized, in 1995, as a World Heritage Site.

As of this writing, no writers had yet been accepted to the Glacier National Park Artist-in-Residency Program, because there were no applicants. Hint, hint.

Matt Graves, Artist-in-Residence Program, Glacier National Park, P.O. Box 128, 1 Going-to-the-Sun Road, West Glacier, Montana 59936, 406-888-7942, matt_graves@nps.gov, www.nps.gov/glac

Grand Canyon National Park
North Rim, Arizona

RESIDENCY: Three-week residencies mid-September to early October, mid-May to early June, and early to mid-July for three writers, visual artists, photographers, performers, video/filmmakers, or composers.

APPLICATION DETAILS: It is important to include only what is required and nothing more, so that your application will be reviewed rather than discarded. Send a list of professional works; a one-page statement of intent that describes the potential of residency for professional growth, the specific focus of your project, the relevancy of your writing and/or proposed project to the natural and cultural resources of Grand Canyon National Park; and a writing sample. The deadline is April 1, no exceptions. A panel consisting of a visual artist, a photographer, a writer, a performing artist or musician, and a multidisciplinary artist will review all entries. Winners are notified by late June.

RESIDENCY REQUIREMENTS: Give two forty-five to sixty-minute formal evening presentations to an audience, informal presentations as work is created, and donate within twelve months after your stay a piece of writing worked on during the residency. The formal and informal presentations will amount to no more than eight hours during the three weeks.

■ **"Draw Your Chair up Close to the Precipice and I'll Tell You a Story"**
F. Scott Fitzgerald was not speaking literally when he said the above quote, but you can when you give your public readings as requirement of staying in a cabin at the North Rim of the Grand Canyon for

three weeks. Ponderosa pine lives with you up at 8,000 feet and above, along with blue spruce, white fir, aspen, mountain ash, Douglas fir, asters, Indian ricegrass, three-awns, blue and black grama, big galleta, groundsels, yarrow, cinquefoil, lupines, blanket flowers, primroses, and sedges. Other elevations include mountain mahogany, elderberry, creeping mahonia, tidy fleabane, Indian paintbrush, sacred datura, desert tobacco, skyrocket, toadflax penstamon, the royal-hued Grand Canyon phacelia, and Rocky Mountain iris.

The Grand Canyon is one of the natural wonders of the world, estimated to be eighteen thousand million years of age, and with raised plateaus and structural basins monopolizing 1,218,375 acres of northern Arizona. It is a semiarid desert with the Colorado river running through it, and its scenic viewpoints at the North Rim are Point Imperial at 8,803 feet, overlooking the Painted Desert and Marble Canyon, with contrasting layers of red and black Precambrian rock; Cape Royal's views of sunrise and sunset, and the Colorado River passing through the natural arch of Angel's Window; Point Sublime at the westernmost tip, hard to reach and offering the loveliest view; and the easily accessible Bright Angel Point, looking out into Roaring Springs and Bright Angel Canyons. The tribes of the area are the Navaho, Havasupai, and Hualapai, all of which are outside the bounds of the park but linked to the land.

If the seasonal rangers are not using the two-room historic cabins dotting a slope beside the chasm, residents get to stay in them; otherwise, you get a like-new, government travel trailer. The "Inn Cabins" are in Transept Canyon behind the grocery store, three-fourths of a mile from the Grand Canyon Lodge, and the trailer is also three-fourths of a mile away but in Norton Court amid ponderosas and aspens. In either case, you have a carpeted bedroom with a queen-size bed, adjoining bathroom with shower, linoleum kitchen with gas stove, refrigerator, table, sink and bench. Bring your own linens. You can choose not to cook in your kitchen and dine at the Lodge, which with its glass defines, once and for all, the "picture window," or drink gourmet coffee and eat pastries at the saloon. You are welcome to bring your family. Forget cell towers and radio waves.

Fredonia, Arizona, is the nearest town, and is sixty miles away on a road that does not have a sixty-mile-an-hour speed limit. Stock up on groceries and bring a cooler for the perishables if you don't have air-conditioning in the car. You can fly a major airline into Phoenix International Airport, take a wee plane up to Flagstaff, then rent a car. Inside the North Rim are a Chevron gas station, a mechanic, and a post office. While neither the cabins nor the travel trailer is accessible to the disabled, the park will make alternate living arrangements for any artist seeking residence who is otherwise qualified.

Greg Litten, Assistant District Interpreter, Artist-in-Residence Program, P.O. Box 129, Grand Canyon, AZ 86023, 928-638-7647, greg_litten@nps.gov, www.nps.gov/gcra

Herbert Hoover National Historic Site
West Branch, Iowa

RESIDENCY: Two to four weeks, May 1 to October 31, for two American writers, composers, or visual or performing artists.

APPLICATION DETAILS: Four copies of a one- to two-page résumé, a summary of creative work (publications, awards), a statement of what you intend to achieve from this residency, a ten-page double-spaced manuscript, and your preferred two- to four-week period of stay. Postmark deadline is March 3, and the selection will be made by March 24.

RESIDENCY REQUIREMENTS: Depending on length of stay, writers present one to two public programs. Donate a piece of work representative of your style and reflective of the residency for the park's museum collection.

■ Prairie Home

Born on August 10, 1874, Herbert Hoover was the son of a Quaker blacksmith and was orphaned early, but he achieved international success as a mining engineer and worldwide gratitude as "The Great Humanitarian" who fed a billion people in fifty-seven countries during and after World War I. And then, after a landslide victory, he became the thirty-first President, and that landslide took him downhill when he couldn't help his countrymen through the Great Depression. But the park is green with life—eighty-one acres of prairie—and a little Quaker town with Friends Meetinghouse, Presidential library and Museum, Hoover's boyhood home, and a blacksmith shop similar to his father's. President and Mrs. Hoover are buried on the historic site. Herbert Hoover National Historic Site was established August 12, 1965. The historic buildings and grounds of this one hundred eighty-six acre site are preserved by the National Park Service.

Residents are provided a large, spacious studio in one of the historic sites or an adjacent facility. As of this writing, no writers have yet been residents, but Park Ranger Dan Peterson says, "We're looking."

Daniel Peterson, Artist-in-Residence Program, Herbert Hoover National Historical Site, P.O. Box 607, West Branch, Iowa 52358, 319-643-2541 ext. 221, dan_peterson@nps.gov, www.nps.gov/heho

"As a poet I wanted to use wildflowers as the 'lens' to look at life, so I applied for a residency in April, peak wildflower season. I hiked the same trails every few days to see the succession of wildflowers in the same place as well as taking cave tours (especially on rainy days), listening to programs offered park visitors, hiking other trails, and talking with park staff and visitors. The self-directed residency gave me the freedom and flexibility to balance the time I spent writing and the time involved in experiencing. Discovering that balance without the confines of domestic responsibility was a large part of the value of the residency."

—Dory Hudspeth, author of *Enduring Wonders* (Word Tech Press, 2007)
and former resident at Mammoth Cave National Park

Hot Springs National Park
Hot Springs, Arkansas

RESIDENCY: Two to four weeks June to November for writers, visual artists, photographers, sculptors, craft artists, video/filmmakers, performers, and composers. The residency must be within a single month, starting on the first, rather than straddling months.

APPLICATION DETAILS: Complete both the Volunteer Application Form 301-A and Authority for Release of Information, which authorizes a police records check, one- to two-page résumé, brief manuscript, a state of intent, and the month you are applying for. A panel of park staff and subject-matter representatives choose finalists based on entry materials, recognized talent, and the artist's ability to relate and interpret the park through their work.

RESIDENCY REQUIREMENTS: Volunteer a few hours to interact with interested park visitors and staff during residency. Donate an original artwork, representative of your style and reflecting your residency, to the park collection.

■ Spa Days

Before the advent of National Parks, Congress established Hot Springs Reservation on April 20, 1832, to protect the forty-seven hot springs flowing from the western slope of Hot Springs Mountain. This predates Yellowstone by forty years, but not until 1921 was its name changed. People have used the hot spring water in therapeutic baths for more than two hundred years to treat rheumatism and other ailments, and the reservation became a resort nicknamed "The American Spa" because it attracted not only the wealthy but also indigent health-seekers from around the world. The park protects the "Bathhouse Row" of eight grand spas, and the surrounding oak-hickory-pine forest ecosystem.

Residents stay in a single-story furnished cabin in Gulpha Gorge Campground that has *seven* rooms—living room, dining room, kitchen, bedroom, bathroom, utility room, and studio—and is outfitted with a washer, dryer, and fully equipped kitchen. The studio has an easel, light table, and true-color light stand and drafting table, so writers who feel the urge to expand their creativity will have the proper equipment. The cabin is not wheelchair accessible.

Artist-in-Residence Program, Hot Springs National Park, P.O. Box 1860, Hot Springs, AR 71902, or Jeff Heitzman, Ranger/Volunteer Coordinator, 501-624-3383 ext. 652, Jeff_heitzman@nps.gov, www.nps.gov/hosp/

Isle Royale National Park
Houghton, Michigan

RESIDENCY: Two to three weeks June through early September for five writers, visual artists, photographers, sculptors, performers, video/film-makers, or composers, annually.

APPLICATION DETAILS: Send a completed application form with writing sample, statement of intent, and résumé. The deadline is February 16.

RESIDENCY REQUIREMENT: Give a talk to park visitors and donate the work you write while in residence.

■ HOWL
Come write and perform your words on a forested island in Lake Superior with timber wolves and moose herds. Explore the pre-Columbian copper mines, shipwrecks, lighthouses, historic fisheries, and resort ruins. Isle Royale is the largest island in Lake Superior, near its north shore, and you pitch a tent on it. Don't worry about the wolves or those tall moose, for they are part of a very rare occurrence—a single-prey, single-predator system. You may run into zoologists, however, come to watch the animals eat each other. It is isolated and beautiful, with one third of the mammalian species of the mainland fifteen miles away.

Established as a National Park in 1940, it was also designated a wilderness in 1976 and an International Biosphere Reserve in 1980. Seaplanes and vessels will get you to the island.

Greg Blust, Artist-in-Residence Program, Isle Royale National Park, 800 East Lakeshore Dr., Houghton, Michigan 49931-1895, 906-487-7152, greg_blust@nps.gov, www.nps.gov/isro/

Mammoth Cave National Park
Mammoth Cave, Kentucky

RESIDENCY: Residencies year-round for local and national writers, artists, and photographers. The park encourages applications for residencies during the spring EARTHSPEAK! activities. There is no application deadline, but spaces are not open every year, so they inquire before applying.

APPLICATION DETAILS: Send a résumé; writing sample; statement of purpose outlining what you hope to accomplish as an artist-in-residence at Mammoth Cave National Park, the specific ideas you have for public interaction and education, and how you and the program will benefit from participation; and a large enough SASE.

RESIDENCY REQUIREMENTSS: Contribute an original finished piece of work representative of your stay at Mammoth Cave National Park. The work will become part of the permanent collection and will be cared for and used by the park in an appropriate manner, and showcased during one of the park's EARTHSPEAK! activities. In addition, artists will have opportunities to sell their works on a limited basis. EARTHSPEAK! encompasses Springfest, which includes the Karstlands Juried Arts Exhibition, and Colorfall, which includes the Colorfall Folkways Exhibition.

■ Seeking Little, Brown and Company
Underneath the Green River Valley and rolling hills of South Central Kentucky is a water-formed labyrinth of caves supporting specialized and interconnected ecosystems. Mammoth is right, as three hundred fifty miles of these caves have been explored and mapped, and suspicions are that one thousand miles exists besides the two hundred other

separate caves. This extraordinary set of caves, interstate karst, forests, glades, stands, barrens, and hills of Mammoth Park, established in 1941, and declared in 1990 an International Biosphere Reserve, are home to more than one hundred thirty species of birds, crustaceans, fish, gastropods, insects, mammals, plants, and reptiles, including mud-puppies, hellbenders, spring peepers, bullfrogs, whippoorwhils, bluegills, eyeless cave fish, troglobitic harvestmen, cave crickets, flying squirrels, stinkpots, big and little bluestem grasses, red cedar, wildflowers, umbrella magnolias, and hemlocks. Among the numerous threatened, endangered, or state-listed species are little brown bats, big brown bats, Indiana bats, Eastern pipistrelles, and Kentucky cave-shrimp.

Artists will be enrolled as Volunteers-in-Parks, and will be covered by workers' compensation for work-related injuries. Be in good health, self-sufficient, and expect to work closely with the park Volunteer Arts Program Coordinator.

Both Louisville, Kentucky, to the north and Nashville, Tennessee, to the south are an hour and a half's drive from the park. Travel options within the park, besides car and your own feet, include horseback, motorbike, and canoe.

Artist-in-Residence Programs, Artist-in-Residence Volunteer, Mammoth Cave National Park, P.O. Box 7, Mammoth Cave, KY 42259, L_Wayne_Johnson@nps.gov/maca, www.nps.gov/maca/

Rocky Mountain National Park
Estes Park, Colorado

RESIDENCY: Two weeks each from early June to late September for writers, artists, composers, and dancers. As a historic site, the cabin is not equipped for those with certain disabilities and can't be altered to become so, though a case-by-case evaluation can be made.

APPLICATION DETAILS: Application form, résumé, a one-page statement of what residency in the Rockies would do for you, and a submission of poems, a story, a novel, or other prose excerpt. Applications can be requested or downloaded off the site. The deadline varies from year to year, but usually is sometime from October through December. Finalists are notified by the end of March. A panel of artists, writers, composers, and dancers review all the applications and come up with five to eight finalists and two alternates.

RESIDENCY REQUIREMENTS: Two public presentations, such as a reading, an exploratory hike, or a lecture, amounting to no more than a few hours out of your stay. Residents donate a piece of writing representative of their stay in the park.

■ Beware of Painters!

The magnificent Rocky Mountain National Park is home to sixty mountains, several waterfalls, marmots, bats, elk, mule deer, moose, falcons, eagles, water ouzels, nutcrackers, black bears, bighorn sheep, coyotes, and painters—also known as mountain lions. For four months, late spring through the end of seasonal summer, the historic William Allen White cabin in Estes Park, at the eastern entrance, houses writers and other artists (painters included) for two-week intervals. Called the "Sun Belt of the Rockies," Estes Park has mild weather with summer day temperatures of 70 to 80 degrees, cooler mountain nights, and, May through August, vibrant wildflowering hills and meadows.

There is only one resident in the rustic William Allen White cabin at a time. Built in 1887 by the Kansas City Star journalist before the establishment in 1915 of the Rocky Mountain National Park, the cabin was assigned to the AIR program in 1984, and has been renovated to include flushing toilets and running water. Situated between evergreens, a snow-powdered peak in the distance, the small, brown cabin has high roof beams and a large fireplace in the living/dining area. The bedroom and bathroom are fully stocked with linens, and the kitchen has pots, pans, utensils, and one of the most valuable writer's tools, a coffee maker. You are welcome to bring a cell phone, though it is not guaranteed to be anything more than a prop of a past life.

The AIR program at Rocky Mountain is one of the founding and longest-running of all the programs in the system and has three aims: to share with the public the scenic beauty and many stories of the Rockies, to preserve the historic William Allen White cabin, and to perpetuate the memory of the man. Rocky takes its AIR program seriously and considers all the artwork, music, and writing donated an important part of the park's heritage, offering a characterization of the environment for all future visitors. Resident writers include Robert Root, Camille Dungy, Xue Di, Carmi Soifer, and Cactus May.

Rocky Mountain National Park offers no stipend, just the full expanse of the park for two weeks and the furnished cabin. Of course, you must bring personal belongings and what you need to write. But you must also purchase your own food from the local Safeway, which means that you must have a car and money for gas. (Most of the splendid park cannot be seen without a car.)

Jean Muenchrath, Supervisory Park Ranger—Interpretation,
Artist-in-Residence Program, Rocky Mountain National Park,

1000 Highway 36, Estes Park, CO 80517, 970-586-1206,
www.nps.gov/romo/visit/park/artist.html

AIR Programs in the Community

Anderson Center for Interdisciplinary Studies
at Tower View
Red Wing, Minnesota

RESIDENCY: The center offers two- to four-week residencies May through October for writers, poets, translators, dancers, archaeologists, painters, composers, historians, folklorists, scholars, photographers, and anthropologists. July is specifically for writers from New York City and all of Minnesota. The application deadline is February 1 for May through July, and March 1 for August through October.

APPLICATION DETAILS: Send a completed application form and a work plan for the project you intend to write and five stapled copies of ten pages of poetry or prose.

RESIDENCY REQUIREMENTS: Give a talk, teach a class, or read your work.

■ Snap, Crackle, Pop
Alexander Pierce Anderson worked on the family farm and as a schoolteacher until a fire burned the house down and his father died. Then

Anderson, who'd always loved biology and zoology, enrolled in the University of Minnesota to study botany, then went for his Ph.D. in Munich. By testing Dr. Heinrich Murray's theory that the central nucleus of a starch granule contains a minuscule amount of condensed water, Anderson heated cornstarch to a very high temperature and caused it to explode. Thus, he created puffed cereal—and secured it over the years with twenty-five patents—and The Anderson Puffed Rice Company. He bought back the family farm, lots more land, built a tower and an estate for his wife and family, and wrote poetry and essays. Anderson believed that fine arts, humanities, and science share common ground, and it is in the light of that philosophy and creative career that The Anderson Center invites interdisciplinary studies from writers, anthropologists, scientists, poets, historians, photographers, translators, dancers, and archaeologists to pop with ideas at Tower View.

Red Wing is an hour's drive from the Twin Cities. You can walk in Thoreau's footsteps up to Barn Bluff, and in early August watch the Dragon Boat races on the Mississippi River.

Anderson Center for Interdisciplinary Studies at Tower View, P.O. Box 406, Red Wing, MN 55066, 651-388-2009, info@andersoncenter.com, www.andersoncenter.com

University of Arizona Poetry Center
Tucson, Arizona

RESIDENCY: The center offers a one-month residency, plus $500 stipend, for an emerging poet, fiction writer, or literary nonfiction writer during June, July, or August. The application period is December 15 to January 15.

APPLICATION DETAILS: Writers at the beginning of their careers, either unpublished or without a full-length book, may apply. Chapbooks are not considered full-length. A self-published book does not count as published. Send three copies of no more than ten pages of poetry or twenty pages of prose and a SASE for reply only. After decisions are made, manuscripts are recycled. There is a $12 reading fee.

RESIDENCY REQUIREMENTS: None

■ **Archival Angel**
The Poetry Center was founded in 1962 after Ruth Stephan's seed collection of several hundred books began to grow into a beautiful noncirculating library. In the 1970s, she and her mother, Myrtle Walgreen, endowed the library with an acquisitions pot of gold, and today it includes more than fifty thousand items, such as single-author monographs, anthologies, literary journals, rare books, limited-edition books, artist-made books, chapbooks, broadsides, photographs, prose and critical works by poets, and reference works. In addition to published recordings, the center's audio/video archive includes recordings that document the Visiting Poets and Writers Reading Series since its inception in 1962. While it was Stephan's intention that the collection emphasize contemporary U.S. poetry, she also stipulated that it include the great poets of all countries in the world. "This is essential," she stated, "in America, whose population is multi-ancestral."

The Center began a residency program in 1993 to support an emerging poet, fiction writer, or literary nonfiction writer each year for one month to develop work and enjoy access to the archives. A new building with climate control is in the works. Residents stay at the University.

University of Arizona Poetry Center, Summer Residency Program,
1600 East 1st Street, Tucson, AZ 85721-0129, 520-626-3765,
poetry@u.arizona.edu, www.poetrycenter.arizona.edu

Note: The following listing was written before the devastation of Hurricane Katrina in the summer of 2005. The proprietors of A Studio in the Woods plan to work with nature to reestablish this residency program. Please continue to check the program's website for improvements.

A Studio in the Woods
New Orleans, Louisiana

RESIDENCY: Four residencies a year for two to four weeks each, available to writers, visual artists, and performing artists September through May.

APPLICATION DETAILS: Seriousness of purpose, harmony with the mission, quality of proposal, creative use of time, space, and environment are considerations for applicants. Send a completed application form, résumé, letter of interest describing how the residency will affect your work/career, the materials you will use and facilities you will need, and how you will know that the time was well-spent. Writers send eight to ten manuscript pages and bibliography and give two references. There's a $20 application fee, and a residency fee of $20 per day to cover food costs for those who are accepted.

RESIDENCY REQUIREMENTS: One public presentation is required during the residency, on- or off-site, and participation in studio tours is optional. You must participate in community dinners, which may include invited guests from the area's artistic community. Writers should donate a piece of writing reflective of their experience for future residents, and write a brief statement on how the residency influenced them personally and artistically.

■ Time-Space Continuum

Artists and environmentalists Lucianne and Joe Carmichael discovered a spot on the west bank of the Mississippi River in the last remaining wetland forest within the city limits of New Orleans in 1969, and have since been restoring the hardwood bottomland forest that was clear-cut in the 1700s for a sugarcane plantation. It's muggy and abuzz with mosquitoes in the semitropical environment. The Carmichaels started offering a room in their rustic homestead as a retreat to artists and in 2002 formed a nonprofit organization and residency program. Here is the gift of time, space, and supportive surroundings in which to experiment and take creative leaps that can result in the great art that allows humankind to extend their vision, awareness, and understanding.

All studio buildings are built with recycled materials with regard to environmental sensitivity. The private guest room on the first floor of the Carmichaels' homestead is air-conditioned. Residents share the living room and kitchen with the Carmichaels and must prepare their own breakfasts. In 2006, there will be accommodations for three or four residents at a time. An air-conditioned studio with a writing desk, easel, and view of the pond in the woods accommodates one writer. Meadows and the river levee can be used for performances. Residents are given lunch and dinner, and vegetarian diets are accommodated. There is a $20 per day fee for food. The site is eight miles from the nearest grocery store, pharmacy, etc., so residents are encouraged to provide their own transportation.

A Studio in the Woods, 13401 River Road, New Orleans, LA 70131, 504-392-5359, 504-394-5977, info@astudiointhewoods.org, www.astudiointhewoods.org

Caldera
Blue Lake, Oregon

RESIDENCY: Caldera offers five two- to four-week residencies at one time for writers and artists November to March. The application deadline is June 1.

APPLICATION DETAILS: Writers and artists with professional standing can apply, as well as those who are emerging and demonstrate promising talent. Send a completed application form and writing sample. All applications are reviewed on a case-by-case basis by an admissions panel, which includes distinguished arts professionals. Former residents may reapply after waiting one year. Notification arrives eight to ten weeks after deadline.

RESIDENCY REQUIREMENTS: A public outreach activity is required, either a workshop in one of Caldera's partner schools or a public presentation of work.

■ **Deschutes! Gesundheit.**
Blue Lake is a caldera—a collapsed volcanic cone that has filled with spring water—in the Cascade Mountains. It is one of the deepest

lakes in Oregon, seventeen miles shy of Sisters, and at an elevation of 3,500 feet. In the winter months, the ninety acres of forestland next to Deschutes National Forest are blanketed with snow, and you can dig a tunnel to your A-frame cottage to write. Inside is a cozy sleeping loft, kitchenette, bathroom and living room/work area. There's baseboard electric heating, a coffeemaker, toaster, microwave, two-burner range and refrigerator, cookware, dishes, towels, bed linens, pillows, and comforters.

The newly completed Hearth Center includes two visual art studios, a four-thousand-square-foot rehearsal/performance space with piano, and a library. You must have a car, possibly even a snowmobile, although the roads are plowed. Caldera will provide wood for your woodstove.

Marna Stalcup, Caldera, 224 NW 13th Ave., Portland, OR 97209, 503-937-7594, marna.stalcup@wk.com, www.caldera.org

Amy Clampitt Residency Program
Stockbridge, Massachusetts

RESIDENCY: The program offers one six- to twelve-month residency, plus stipend, for an emerging or established poet or literary scholar annually.

APPLICATION DETAILS: Send a résumé; a letter of no more than two pages describing your interest in the residency and the work you propose to undertake, and which six- to twelve-month period, August to July, you would like to have; a ten-page representative work sample completed in the last four years; and three personal and professional references.

RESIDENCY REQUIREMENTS: A local, public reading during the residency.

■ Late Bloom

The lake country of the Berkshire Hills was home to the poet Amy Clampitt, whose first full-length collection, *The Kingfisher*, was published by Alfred A. Knopf when she was in her fifties. Thanks to the estate of her husband, Harold Korn, who established the Amy Clampitt Fund, the three-bedroom cottage in Stockbridge can be a temporary home to a poet or literary scholar once a year. A resident receives a $2,500 stipend for each month. The Cape-style house is fully furnished with a phone line and DSL in a quiet residential neighborhood a few minutes' walk from the village of Lenox. Partners and children can accompany the resident.

Iowan Amy Clampitt wrote often of birds, blooms, and water, and was for years a librarian at the Audubon Society in New York City. Knopf published all her books, including *What the Light Was Like*, *Archaic Figure*, and *Westward. A Silence Opens*. With part of the sum Clampitt received as MacArthur Fellow in 1992, she bought her small two-story house and lived there until her death in 1994. The Amy Clampitt Fund seeks to benefit poetry and the literary arts by converting the house into a facility that provides for a place to foster the study and promotion of poetry and/or a poet-in-residence. It is housed at Berkshire Taconic Community Foundation, a nonprofit organization that cultivates philanthropy in ways that have a direct positive impact in Berkshire, Columbia, Northeast Dutchess, and Northwest Litchfield counties. Begun in 2003, Willard Spiegelman and Alfred Corn were the first and second residents.

Berkshire Taconic Community Foundation, 271 Main St., Suite 3, Great Barrington, MA, 800-969-2823, www.berkshire-taconic.org

AWAY TO WRITE

Ironically, going away to write in a remote artist colony for one to six months is easy in our technological age. Cell phones will be useless and Internet connections rare, but you can pay all your bills with online banking before you leave home, set up a vacation message on your e-mail program, and finish your novel in a cabin situated in wildflowering mountains. These are casual environments, but you may want to bring one item that dresses you up, should there be a trip to town for theater. Writers-in-residence in colleges should bring teaching attire. Pack according to the climate, allergens, and terrain, as well as your comfort. I was right to bring a Walkman for music to soothe me to sleep in a dark, quiet mountain cabin with gargoyles carved into the bedroom furniture, but I did not end up needing the snakebite kit at Dorland Mountain Arts Colony. Garlic capsules—which are tasteless—will keep mosquitoes and other biting insects away without chemicals. Arnica gel will erase bruises and their pain.

Janice Eidus sends boxes of books to MacDowell or Yaddo when she goes for six weeks so that she can catch up on her reading as well as her writing. Monique Truong carefully selects which CDs to bring, and other writers send ahead other touchstones of their writing environments. When you go away to write, you are leaving behind distractions, arguments, and, let's face it, people in your life. But not everyone is more prolific alone. Poets Nick Carbo and Denise Duhamel write better when they are in each other's company. They have stayed together at every colony they have been to while married. They either apply for the same time period and notify the colony or, for programs in foreign countries, such as Civatella Ranieri in the Tuscan region of Italy, hang out in the same castle chamber.

Hidden River Arts
Bethany, Delaware

RESIDENCY: Four two-week residencies at one time, December to February and March to May for writers of plays, fiction, nonfiction, and poetry. The application period is August 1 to September 15 for fall/winter residencies.

APPLICATION DETAILS: Send a completed application form with a writing sample (fifteen pages of a play with a one-page synopsis, twenty-five pages of fiction and nonfiction, or ten pages of poetry); a brief bio; a project description and also briefly how residency at this point would support your work; a résumé; and the $15 application fee. Name your first, second, and third choice of weeks to stay.

■ From Obscure to Hidden
Hidden River Arts is an independent nonprofit literary arts organization based in suburban Philadelphia and named after the Schuylkill (Dutch for "Hidden River"), which winds its way through the region. Hidden River Arts is committed to nurturing the artistic community by providing varied and supportive services to creative writers who find their voices outside the MFA programs, finishing their novels while working at their day jobs. They look for the creative talent that is grown, nurtured, and matured in the kiln of real-life experience. It is their belief that many, many talented writers go unheard because they labor in obscurity or isolation, dispersed throughout the nonacademic population with little or no support for the practice of their art. They reach out to those far-flung voices with programs and contests, and a writer-in-residency program on Bethany Beach in Delaware.

Debra Leigh Scott, Founding Director, Hidden River Arts, P.O. Box 421,
Bala Cynwyd, PA 19004-0421, info@hiddenriverarts.org,
www.hiddenriverarts.org

Isabella Stewart Gardner Museum
Boston, Massachusetts

RESIDENCY: Five one-month residencies plus travel and stipend year-round for writers, storytellers, visual artists, photographers, sculptors, composers, performing artists. The application deadline is September 29.

APPLICATION DETAILS: Send the completed application form with preferences for residency dates, a short-form curriculum vitae, a one-page description of the project, three reference letters, and a writing sample, submitted in triplicate.

RESIDENCY REQUIREMENT: Schedule permitting, the artist-in-residence works with the museum's education department to teach area school-children for at least twelve hours during the residency term.

■ Garden of Delight
Come live, explore, and respond to this museum's thirty centuries of art, unique installations, architectural beauty, and rich archives. Three floors of intimate, personal galleries surround a blooming garden courtyard. Isabella and her husband, Jack, started the collection of paintings, sculptures, tapestries, furniture, and decorative arts in their residence, and later began planning a museum. After Jack's death, Isabella bought land in Fenway Park. The museum has always been home to artists, writers, and thinkers from the world over, from John

Singer Sargent to Okakuro Kakuzo, and still is with its residency program. The resident lives in an apartment on the premises, and has expert, guided access to all the art for the month of their stay. The museum provides round-trip airplane tickets at a discounted coach fare, a housing stipend of $50 per day, and a general stipend of $7,000. Writers have included Ann Nivat, Gcina Mhlophe, and Alessandero Baricco.

Isabella Stewart Gardner Museum, 2 Palace Road, Boston, MA 02115, 617-278-5108, contemporary@isgm, www.isgm.org

The Island Institute
Sitka, Alaska

RESIDENCY: One-month residencies plus stipend in January, April, and November for writers and humanities scholars whose work demonstrates an interest in the integration of the arts, humanities, and sciences. The application deadline is April 15 for the following November or the following January or April.

APPLICATION DETAILS: Send a completed application form and three copies of a sample of recent writing of ten pages of poetry or twenty pages of prose, a résumé, one or two paragraphs on the work you plan to do in Alaska, and three letters of reference, including two from authorities in your field.

RESIDENCY REQUIREMENTS: Residents give a reading, teach a workshop, give a talk, contribute to discussions, visit school classes, or do some other community activity.

■ **Wonderland**

The Island Institute fosters insight, moral compass, and right action, and celebrates the diversity of the world's inhabitants. Sitka is on the coast of Baronof Island, at the same latitude as London, and is home to the Tlingit Indians. The Institute relies on wonder to open eyes and ears and cultivate a sympathetic imagination, and their 2005 Sitka Symposium asked: If this is your land, where are your stories? Residents pay for travel, and the institute pays a stipend that covers housing and food. Recent fellows include Brendan Jones, Christopher Matthews, Stefani Harris, and Patricia Klindienst.

The Island Institute, P.O. Box 2420, Sitka, AK 99835, 907-747-3794, island@ak.net, www.islandinstitutealaska.org

Thurber House
Columbus, Ohio

RESIDENCY: Two four-week residencies with stipend available, ordinarily one for writers of adult fiction and one for emerging writers of children's literature, during the months of June and July. In 2005, the adult fiction residency was put on hiatus while Thurber House reorganized.

APPLICATION DETAILS: Inquire about the adult fiction writer-in-residency program; new guidelines will become available after they restructure the program. Publishers nominate authors for the children's author residency, so pick up the phone and call your editor.

RESIDENCY REQUIREMENT: Children's authors teach children ten hours a week at the summer camp, and writers of adult fiction teach classes at the Thurber House, too.

■ The Night the Bed Fell

Resident writers get to stay in an apartment in the third-floor attic where James Thurber's grandfather slept—and his father, too, on one fateful night—for a quiet living and working environment at this literary center located in the historic former home of author, humorist, and *New Yorker* cartoonist James Thurber. Thurber House is a living museum, furnished in the style of the 1913–1917 period when the author lived here with his parents, two brothers, and several canine companions (*Thurber's Dogs*). There's even a trove of ghost stories you can add to if you are (un)lucky.

Thurber House sponsors an award for humorists, summer literary picnics, summer camp for children, book groups, and other programs. Columbus is an artistic and cultural city with theater, music, museums, and literary events.

Martha Miller, Thurber House, 77 Jefferson Ave., Columbus, OH 43215, 614-464-1032, Patricia Shannon: pshannon@thurberhouse.org, www.thurberhouse.org

Writers Colony at Dairy Hollow
Eureka Springs, Arkansas

RESIDENCY: Five residencies at a time for writers (including food writers) and composers to stay two to eight weeks February to November. General residency and dedicated fellowships are available. There is no actual application deadline; writers may apply at any time.

APPLICATION DETAILS: Applications can be completed online or sent in. Send in a completed application form; brief proposed description of writing you will work on; lists of your publications, professional achievements, honors, awards, contests, prizes, and professional education; ten-page writing sample; two references; and the $35 fee.

RESIDENCY REQUIREMENT: For each thirty days of residency, writers commit to a minimum of one day of community service. This can be workshops, seminars, readings, or other forms of interaction. Books by residents are always a welcome donation. All writers, regardless of length of stay, are welcome and encouraged to do so. The staff actively assists in organizing public events.

■ Feeling Hollow or Fried?

The American Egg Board sponsors one of the many fellowships for writer's residencies at Dairy Hollow, nearly half of which support culinary writers. Though within the city limits of Eureka Springs, in the Ozark Mountains, the colony is nestled in a private wooded hollow, adjacent to a park and near walking and biking paths that lead to Beaver Lake and the White River. If you apply outside of the fellowships, you must donate money—as little as $20—to the colony.

You will have a private room and bath in a shared facility, with linens. Dinner is prepared five nights per week and vegetarian meals are available. A stocked kitchen is available for residents to prepare their own breakfast and lunch, and with all those food writers, you'll never be bored. The common room is for residents' use, and laundry facilities are on-site. You can get Internet connection only in the residents' area, but you'll have to use your own computer. Public transportation is available in the form of a trolley system. Smokers must go outdoors.

The Writers Colony at Dairy Hollow, 515 Spring St., Eureka Springs, AR 72632, 501-253-7444 (tel.), 501-253-9859 (fax), director@writerscolony.org, www.writerscolony.org

Academic Writer-in-Residency Programs

Bucknell University
$4,000 Philip Roth Residence in Creative Writing
Lewisberg, Pennsylvania

Poets and fiction writers are eligible to spend the fall semester at Bucknell to complete a first or second book, interact with students, and give a public reading. Lodging and an office at The Stadler Center for Poetry is provided. Send a letter of application, curriculum vitae, three references, and no more than ten pages of poetry or twenty pages of prose. Alternate years for poetry and prose. The award is named after Philip Roth, the major American novelist, author of *Goodbye, Columbus*, *Portnoy's Complaint*, and *American Pastoral*, and other novels.

Philip Roth Residence in Creative Writing, The Stadler Center for Poetry, Bucknell Hall, Bucknell University, Lewisburg, PA 17837

Lynchburg College
$8,000 Thornton Writer Residency
Lynchburg, Virginia

Poets, novelists, dramatists, and nonfiction writers with teaching experience can come to work on a project, teach an eight-week class, and give readings for one semester. The fall semester is for fiction, and spring is for poets. Housing, meals, and roundtrip airfare are included. Send a book, curriculum vitae, and cover letter detailing your teaching experience by March 1.

Thornton Writer Residency, Lynchburg College, 1501 Lakeside Dr., Lynchburg, VA 24501, www.lynchburg.edu/academics/english/index.htm

Phillips Exeter Academy
$10,000 George Bennett Fellowship
Exeter, New Hampshire

Fiction writers, preferably, poets, and nonfiction writers who have not yet published a book are eligible to come work on a project for one academic year and be informally available to talk with students who are interested in writing. Housing and meals are provided for the writer and family. Send application, two references, a statement of purpose, fifty pages of fiction or twenty to thirty pages of poetry, and the $5 application fee. The deadline is December 1.

Bennett Fellowship, Phillips Exeter Academy, 20 Main St., Exeter, NH 03833-2460

Princeton University
$56,000 Alfred Hodder Fellowship
Princeton, New Jersey

Writers, preferably outside academia, who have already published one highly acclaimed book are eligible to apply. Recipients live in Princeton and work on independent projects at the Joseph Henry

House for one academic year. Send résumé, ten pages of writing, a two- to three-page project proposal, and an SASE. Alfred Hodder was an attorney and author of three books, including the novel *The New Americans*, published in 1901.

Alfred Hodder Fellowship, Joseph Henry House, Princeton University, Princeton, NJ 08544-5264

Radcliffe College
$55,000 Bunting Fellowship Program
Cambridge, Massachusetts

Writers, scholars, scientists, and artists of exceptional promise and demonstrating accomplishment, who wish to pursue work in academic and professional fields and in the creative arts are eligible to apply. Residents live in the Boston area and get studio space at the institute, a computer with high-speed Internet access, and the libraries and other resources of Harvard. Send four copies of the application form, a curriculum vitae, a project proposal, a thirty-page writing sample, and one copy of financial information. The deadline is October 3. The Institute is concerned with women, gender, and society but supports both women and men.

Fellowship Program, Radcliffe Institute, 34 Concord Ave., Cambridge, MA 02138, 617-495-8212, fellowship@radcliffe.edu

Stanford University
$56,000 Wallace Stegner Fellowships
Stanford, California

Five poets and five fiction writers can come to write and attend workshops for two academic years at Stanford in the company of their peers and the guidance of accomplished writers. Send a brief statement of your writing plans; ten to fifteen pages of poetry and a short story and a novel excerpt or a novel excerpt not to exceed 9,000 words, mailing labels, and an SASE. Wallace Stegner founded Stanford University.

Stegner Fellowships, Creative Writing Department, Stanford University, Stanford, CA 94305, www.stanford.edu/dept/english/cw

---

"In Madison, I not only made great friends with some of the other fellows (there are six at any time) but also had the advantages of being connected to a major research institution. I was able to meet a Ph.D. in botany who specialized in palynology on pacific islands—the same as my novel's main character! I interviewed her, spent time in her lab, and ended up setting a section of my novel at the University of Wisconsin."

—Jennifer Vanderbes, author of *Easter Island* and McCreight Fellow at The University of Wisconsin

---

University of Wisconsin, Madison
The Wisconsin Institute for Creative Writing
$25,000 Carl Djerassi, Diane Middlebrook,
James C. McCreight, Carol Houck Smith,
and Jay C. & Ruth Halls Fellowships
Madison, Wisconsin

Three poets and three fiction writers who have completed their MFA or Ph.D. degrees in creative writing but have not yet published a book are eligible to live for one academic year in Madison and work at the Institute, teach one creative writing course each semester, and give one public reading from the work-in-progress. Send ten pages of poetry or one story of up to thirty pages during February. Also send résumé or curriculum vitae, two references, a $20 application fee, and an SASE.

Jesse Lee Kercheval, Wisconsin Institute for Creative Writing, Department of English, 600 N. Park St., University of Wisconsin, Madison, WI 53706

5 Grants and Fellowships

Once you've lived in a state for two or three years, and have written at least ten pages of polished poetry or one superior story, you're qualified to apply for grants and fellowships. And let me tell you that the State Arts Councils are calling out to writers, looking under rocks for you, behind trees in the hide-and-seek forest. It is their mission to support you and the other artistic folk in your home state. They are the most lenient in the application process, which means that you can do well only by trying. Regional arts councils offer grants, too, quite often in the form of Special Opportunity Stipends (SOS), and you can apply for money to take a workshop with your idol in the poetry world or to pay for childcare while you go to a library to quietly write another chapter of your novel. For these, you need to present a budget and the fact of a workshop held somewhere. What's more, state, regional, and city arts councils often hold free seminars once a month before fellowship deadlines to go over how to put together the best application.

This process is really habit-forming. Some of the grants out there are for writers who have already published a book that has been well-reviewed, but there are many others open to anyone with a good project. If you have just obtained your MFA degree, then you probably are ready to venture forth into the world of grants. However, you do not need an MFA degree to apply to grants and fellowships. The writing is what will win a grant for you, so be sure that you choose the very best work to send the foundations. They organize panels of readers that either change yearly or remain in place for a block of years. If the panels change, you must reapply the following year—unless you won—but even if they remain the same, your manuscript might rise to the top of a different stack. Continue to polish your writing by attending artists colonies and residencies, and continue to send it out for grants and fellowships. Don't give up!

I am not including all state arts councils in this book. They are on the accompanying CD-ROM, along with more travel, research, project, and regional grants. What is here is a mix of opportunities for emerging and more established writers, and the emergency money sources available to qualified writers in the know. Most organizations and foundations that offer emergency money do not have websites or information about their emergency grants on websites. You must call or write for information.

Grants and Fellowships

American Academy in Berlin
New York, New York

$3,000 to $5,000 Berlin Prize monthly stipend for writers, poets, journalists, artists, composers, and scholars.

APPLICATION DETAILS: Send five copies of the completed application form with a project proposal that includes a description, work plan, how the residency will help you, and what form your project will take; a curriculum vitae; and two published chapters or articles. The deadline is October 17.

The Berlin Prize is prestigious, and the writers who have won are accomplished and well reviewed. The prize includes round-trip airfare, partial board, and monthly stipend for a semester. Residents stay in a generous apartment at the Hans Arnhold Center, a historic lakeside villa in the Wannsee district of Berlin. Recipients come from academic, cultural, and public-affairs backgrounds and work on novels, poetry collections, nonfiction, literary criticism, and journalism. The center arranges lectures, conferences, exhibits, and concerts throughout the year so that fellows can exchange ideas and experiences. Past recipients include W. S. Di Piero, Jeffrey Eugenides, Elizabeth Mc-Cracken, Sigrid Nunez, and C. K. Williams.

The American Academy in Berlin is a private, nonprofit center for advanced study that with its Berlin Prize Fellowships creates a bridge between Germany and America through scholarship and creativity. Banker and cultural leader Hans Arnhold, whose villa is now the center, fled Germany in the 1930s, after which Walther Funk, Third Reich Minister of Finance, claimed the villa. Later, it was a city home for refugees from the east, sold to the Federal Republic of Germany and remodeled, and used as a U.S. Army recreation center. Finally, a founding gift of Anna-Maria and Stephen M. Kellen and the family of Hans and Ludmilla Arnhold renovated the villa for the American Academy in Berlin, which began its work there in September 1998.

American Academy in Berlin, New York Office, 14 E. 60th St., Suite 604, New York, NY 10022, 212-588-1755, nyoffice@americanacademy.de, www.americanacademy.de

---

"The National Endowment for the Arts Fellowship provided time and space to finish a poetry manuscript called *Fieldnotes*. I took two summers off from teaching to travel the Great Plains, to read the necessary books, to research, to think, to write, to rewrite, to send out individual poems, to arrange and rearrange them in a collection. The NEA helped me cover ground. It was the underwriter for my project. It gave me a sense of authenticity. An NEA is gravy. It is release. It is writing time and gas money. For me, the land carries words. It carries the native voice. It carries the past. It was in travel that I found the particular voice for this book with acknowledgment to the NEA."

—Diane Glancy

American Antiquarian Society (AAS)
Worcester, Massachusetts

$1,200 Creative and Performing Artists Writers Fellowships for fiction writers, poets, playwrights, screenwriters, nonfiction writers, filmmakers, and performing artists.

APPLICATION DETAILS: Send a cover sheet; two letters of recommendation; a current résumé; a statement summarizing educational and professional background and goals, describing the research for the project including readings in primary and secondary sources, and indicating the nature of the research program proposed for the AAS fellowship; and ten copies of a representative sample of previous writing, no more than twenty-five double-spaced pages. The Society's goal in sponsoring this program is to multiply and improve the ways in which an understanding of history is communicated to the American people. The deadline is October 5.

The Creative and Performing Artists Writers Fellowships are project grants involving research concerning pre-twentieth-century American history, and are open to emerging and established writers working on historical novels, poetry, articles, nonfiction works of history, children's books, and other imaginative, nonformulaic projects for a general readership. The American Antiquarian Society is a national research library and learned society of American history and culture that awards at least three fellows a four-week residency at the society for uninterrupted research, reading, and collegial discussion, and $1,200 for travel and room and board. Fellows have included Amy Brill, Geoffrey Brock, Nicole Cooley, Joann Dobson, Camille Dungy, John Lee, Catherine Gammon, Jeanne Mackin, Sarah Messer, and Cornelia Nixon.

Creative and Performing Artists Writers Fellowship, American Antiquarian Society, 185 Salisbury St., Worcester, MA 01609, 708-755-5221, www.americanantiquarian.org

A Room of Her Own
Placitas, New Mexico

$50,000 Gift of Freedom Award for women poets, fiction writers, and creative nonfiction writers.

APPLICATION DETAILS: Send a well-articulated creative project concept and a clear plan for how it may accomplished. The form of submission to A Room of Her Own varies with the artist's chosen field, but an essay on your artistic life, a sample of writing, and a record of your community service, educational background, and employment history is required, as well as complete disclosure of data and assets. The next award cycle, in fall of 2006, will be for fiction. Inquire in 2006 for deadline information.

This is a fantastic—in the true sense of the word—project grant for a woman with a social and artistic vision who has solid creative goals and a specific project to accomplish during the two-year term of the grant, or who has a track record of commitment to her art and making a substantial effort to be self-sufficient. An award recipient has a "moral" contract to complete her project and give back to A Room of Her Own Foundation and mentor other Gift of Freedom recipients. Past recipients include the poet Jennifer Tseng and creative nonfiction writer Meridith Hall.

The novelist Virginia Woolf famously said, "A woman must have money and a room of her own if she is to write." A Room of Her

Own Foundation is a nonprofit organization founded in 2000 to further the vision of Woolf by bridging the often fatal gap between a woman's economic reality and her artistic creation. They provide innovative and practical arts patronage to women through their generous grant program and unique retreats at Georgia O'Keefe's Ghost Ranch in New Mexico. They hope to create educational programs that instruct the public about the needs and contributions of women artists, including visits to schools and other educational opportunities in the broader community.

A Room of Her Own, Box 778, Placitas, NM 87043,
info@aroomofherownfoundation.org,
www.aroomofherownfoundation.org

Arrowhead Regional Arts Council
Duluth, Minnesota

$2000 to $4000 McKnight/ARAC Individual Artist Fellowships to recognize, reward, and encourage literary, visual, and performing artists.

APPLICATION DETAILS: You will need to send in the completed grant application form, the completed RAC Data Collection form, a fellowship work plan in narrative form of no more than two pages, an artistic résumé of no more than two pages, a work sample, and return postage. The work plan should cover your artistic direction, what the money would afford you to do, and how it impacts your goals as well as a budget. There should be an artist statement at the top of your artistic résumé, and then headings, where applicable, for education, publications, employment, honors, awards, and memberships. The work sample should be up to ten pages single-spaced of poetry, up to twenty pages double-spaced of fiction or creative nonfiction, and up to twenty-five pages double-spaced for plays. The deadline is late March.

The McKnight/ARAC Individual Artist Fellowship Program is open to emerging playwrights, poets, fiction and creative nonfiction writers, visual artists, and performers who are U.S. citizens and residents of Aitkin, Carlton, Cook, Itasca, Koochiching, Lake, and St. Louis counties. By awarding four fellowships for $4,000 and two fellowships for $2,000, the program enables writers to set aside time to work to achieve specific career goals, participate in advanced study not related to a degree program, or to pursue other activities that will allow them to meet their creative goals. Funding for the Artist Fellowships comes from the Minnesota State Legislature and the McKnight Foundation.

Arrowhead Regional Arts Council, Robert DeArmond, Executive Director, Marshall School Annex Building, 1301 Rice Lake Road, Suite 111, Duluth, MN 55811, 218-722-0952, ARACouncil@aol.com, www.aracouncil.org

Artist Trust
Seattle, Washington

$6,000 WSCA Fellowships to Washington State residents. $1,400 Grants for Artist Projects (GAP) for Washington State residents.

APPLICATION DETAILS: WSCA Fellowship applications are available in April. For GAP, submit six three-hole punched copies of application form and budget page, one three-hole punched copy of résumé, six three-hole punched copies of work sample description, and six copies of an eight-page work sample secured with binder clips. Include an SASE. The deadline is February 24 for GAP and June 24 for WSCA Fellowships.

GAP awards support the development, completion, or presentation of new work, and offer a maximum of $1,400 for projects. In 2004, forty artists won GAP awards, including eight writers. Artist Trust/Washington State Arts Commission Fellowships for $6,000 are, by contrast, merit-based and given in two-year cycles to artists of exceptional talent and demonstrated ability. Writers may apply in even-numbered years. Applicants to either must be practicing artists eighteen years or older, and residents of Washington at the time of application and award.

Artist Trust provides vital financial support through its grants programs and information services to artists working in all disciplines throughout Washington State. In fact, 1,112 artists have received 2.2 million dollars of grant support since 1986. Besides the GAP Program and the WSCA Fellowships, Artist Trust administers the Twining Humber Award for Visual Artists, offers information services for artists throughout the state, and publishes a triannual newsletter, *The Journal.*

Fionn Meade, Director of Grant Programs, Artist Trust, 1402 Third Ave., Suite 404, Seattle, WA 98101-2118, info@artisttrust.org, www.artisttrust.org

Astraea Foundation
Lesbian Writers Fund
New York, New York

$100 to $10,000 grants to support emerging lesbian poets and fiction writers.

APPLICATION DETAILS: You must send a cover sheet and application form with a $5 processing fee. Winners are notified in the summer. The deadline is February 15.

These grants are given to support writers of work with some lesbian content, who are in the early stages of their careers, with as little as one piece published in a newspaper, magazine, journal, Web publication, or anthology, and no more than one book published. Four $10,000 grants are awarded, two in each category, two $1,500 runners-up, and six $100 honorable mentions.

Founded by Joan Drury, the Astraea Lesbian Foundation for Justice works for social, racial, and economic justice in the United States and internationally through grant-making and philanthropic advocacy programs to help lesbians and allied communities challenge oppression and claim their human rights. Since 1991, they have awarded nearly half a million dollars to emerging poets and fiction writers across the United States. In 2005, $26,600 went to twelve women. Recent winners include Samiya Bashir, Debra Busman, Jenna Capeci, Kirsten Dinall Hoyt, Meg Jochild, and Lu Vickers.

Astraea Foundation, Lesbian Writers Fund, 116 E. 16 St., New York, NY 10003, www.astraea.org

Bronx Council on the Arts

Bronx, New York

$2,500 Bronx Recognizes Its Own (BRIO) Fellowships for literary artists, visual artists, performing artists, and media artists.

APPLICATION DETAILS: Send five copies of a typed manuscript of twenty double-spaced pages prose and plays or ten pages single-spaced poetry created in the last five years. You must be eighteen years or older, and a Bronx resident. The deadline is mid-January.

The BRIO Fellowships are beginner grants for writers in the borough of the Bronx. Since the New York State Council on the Arts does not award individual artist fellowships, this fellowship program is vital in recognizing a community that is predominantly Latino. Recipients must complete a onetime public-service activity to receive their award. Winners include Bob Cohen, Aldina Vazao Kennedy, Sarah Stern, Elizabeth Bassford, Baruch Israel, and James McSherry.

The Bronx Council on the Arts has been the official cultural agency of Bronx County for more than forty years and is a private, nonprofit membership organization serving a multicultural community of more than 1.2 million residents. Their mission is to encourage and increase the public's awareness and participation in the arts, and to nurture the development of artists and arts and cultural organizations.

BRIO Fellowships, The Bronx Council on the Arts, 1738 Hone Ave., Bronx, NY 10461-1486, 718-931-9500, Bronxarts@bronxarts.org, www.bronxarts.org

Bronx Writers' Center
Bronx, New York

$5,000 BWC Literary Arts Fellowship and Residency for poets, fiction writers, playwrights, and screenwriters under the age of thirty.

APPLICATION DETAILS: Submit four copies of a manuscript created in the last five years; prose writers submit up to twenty pages, double-spaced, and poets submit up to ten pages, single-spaced. The deadline is late June.

These fellowships are a great opportunity for writers under the age of thirty to find the extra money that affords more time for writing and professional development. They are more competitive than the BRIO awards because they are open to writers of poetry, fiction, plays, and screenplays from all five boroughs of New York City. This is not a strict community residency; the winners must only perform a public-service project at The Bronx Writers' Center during their year of the fellowship, and will receive their grant money as a monthly stipend.

The Bronx Writers' Center is supported by The Bronx Council on the Arts and the New York State Council on the Arts, and provides a variety of programs, readings, workshops, and awards to emerging writers in the Bronx and New York City. The deadline is late June.

Bronx Writers' Center Fellowship, c/o The Bronx Writers' Center, 2521 Glebe Ave., Bronx, NY 10461-1486, www.bronxarts.org/gp_bwc

CEC International Partners
New York, New York

$2,500 to $10,000 Artslink Collaborative Projects between writers, visual artists, media artists, dancers, or actors in the United States and those in Central Europe, Russia, and Eurasia.

APPLICATION DETAILS: Send in a completed application form; a project description and timeline of no more than one page; the answers to six questions, in two to three pages, having to do with artistic vision, overseas partnership, cross-cultural challenges, and resources; a letter of invitation from a Central European, Russian, or Eurasian artist or organization describing their participation in the project; a curriculum vitae or résumé of no more than two pages; and an SASE for receipt of application materials. Literary artists can apply in even-numbered years. The deadline is mid-January.

These grants are for U.S. artists in literature, the performing arts, and visual and media arts. ArtsLink Projects allow for individuals, as well as for curators, presenters, and nonprofit arts organizations, to undertake projects that draw inspiration from interaction with artists in Central Europe, Russia, and Eurasia.

CEC ArtsLink is an international arts service organization that considers the arts society's aims to help nations overcome long histories of reciprocal distrust, insularity, and conflict. It sponsors many programs and awards, and since 1993 has supported two hundred seventy-four ArtsLink Projects in twenty-three countries. The five individual literature winners since 1999 have been playwrights and poets, and include Lisa Schlensinger from Iowa City, Iowa, who taught a playwriting workshop with Andras Nagy to emerging women playwrights in Budapest, Hungary, and H. L. Hix of Kansas City, Missouri, who traveled to Estonia to work with Dr. Juri Talvet, Head of the Department of Literature at the University of Tartu on the translation of contemporary Estonian poetry into English for an anthology.

CEC International Partners, 435 Hudson St., 8th Fl., New York, NY 10014, 212-643-1985, al@cecartslink.org, www.cecArtsLink.org

Cintas Foundation
New York, New York

$10,000 Cintas Fellowships to Cuban writers, artists, musicians, and architects.

APPLICATION DETAILS: Send the application form, a narrative artist's statement, a narrative project statement, two letters of recommendation, and a work sample. Writers should submit two copies of one original manuscript or portion of a manuscript, no more than twenty-five numbered pages. One sample publication may also accompany the manuscript but should not be submitted in lieu of the manuscript. The deadline is February 18.

These fellowships are given to writers, architects, musicians, and artists of direct Cuban lineage or citizenship who are currently living outside of Cuba. Previous winners include Reinaldo Arinas, Lourdes Blanco, Silvia Curbelo, Margarita Engle, Maria Irene Fornes, Oscar Hijuelos, Ricardo Paul Llosa, Pablo Medina, and Alina Troyano.

Oscar B. Cintas was a former Cuban ambassador to the United States in the early 1930s, and a prominent industrialist and patron of the arts. The Cintas Fellowship Program is administered by the Cintas Foundation Board and the Institute of International Education, the nation's oldest and most active organization in the field of international education and cultural exchange—also responsible for the Fulbright Scholarship.

Jose W. Perez, Program Manager, Cintas Foundation, Frost Art Museum at Florida International University, 11200 SW 8 St., PC 110, Miami, FL 33199, 305-348-6086, perezjos@fiu.edu, www.cintasfoundation.org

John Simon Guggenheim Memorial Foundation
New York, New York

$37,000 to scholars and writers of poetry, plays, screenplays, fiction, and creative nonfiction.

APPLICATION DETAILS: Send a completed application form and two copies each of three statements: a brief narrative account of your career, describing accomplishments such as prizes, honors, or grants and fellowships (dates and grantors included); a detailed list of publications or productions; and a brief statement of plans for the period of the fellowship. Send samples of published writing (no more than three different books and two copies of the most recent of these) and a list of the books submitted. Applications become available in July of each year, and final selections are made in April. The deadline is October 1 for U.S. and Canadian applicants.

The Guggenheim Fellowships are prestigious; they open doors—electric garage doors; sleek, racecar doors—and are awarded to those who have demonstrated exceptional creativity. Most writers who apply have at least one book published or play produced and a smattering of other accolades. The average award is just over $37,000 for a period of six months to a year. There are two annual competitions, one for the United States and Canada, and one for Latin America and the Caribbean. All applicants must be citizens or permanent residents of the eligible countries. Past fellows may not reapply.

The 2005 winners include Kim Addonizio, Sarah Arvio, Blake Bailey, Jo Ann Beard, Adam Haslett, Fanny Howe, Pico Iyer, Rohinton Mistry, Harryette Mullen, ZZ Packer, Spencer Reece, and Jim Shepard.

Senator and Mrs. Simon Guggenheim created the John Simon Guggenheim Memorial Foundation in 1925 to honor their son John who had passed away. The Foundation gives fellowships to scholars and writers by helping them to engage in research in any field and to create in any of the arts under the freest possible conditions and irrespective of race, color, or creed.

John Simon Guggenheim Memorial Foundation, 90 Park Ave., New York, NY 10016, 212-687-4470, 212-687-3248, fellowships@gf.org, www.gf.org

Institute for International Education
Fulbright Scholar Program
New York, New York

APPLICATION DETAILS: Your statement of proposed research or study should include your reasons for choosing a particular country; the form your work will take, and the expected results; the contribution that a foreign experience will have on your future professional development; host country affiliations; and where possible, letters of support. Inquire about the specifics of the writing sample. The deadlines are May 1 and October 21. The submission period is May 1 to October 21.

This program helps creative writers and journalists to carry out a major writing project overseas. The Fulbright awards winners round-trip transportation to the host country, maintenance for the academic year, minimal book and research allowances, supplemental health and accident insurance, tuition (in some cases), and language or orientation classes.

Established in 1946, the Fulbright Program aims to increase mutual understanding between the United States and other countries.

Fulbright Scholar Program, Institute of International Education, U.S. Student Programs Division, 809 United Nations Plaza, New York, NY 10017, www.iie.org

The Jerome Foundation Travel and Study Grant Program
Saint Paul, Minnesota

$4,000 for U.S. travel or $5,000 for foreign travel to Minnesota artists and arts organizations, including literary and dramatic arts for a period of significant professional development through travel and study. The deadline is February.

American painter, musician, and filmmaker Jerome Hill was born in Saint Paul, Minnesota, to an artist and art collecting father who was heir to the Great Northern Railroad fortune. The Jerome Foundation is the second foundation, after The Camargo Foundation, that Hill started to support artists and arts organizations in New York City and Minnesota.

Travel and Study Grant Program, The Jerome Foundation, 400 Sibley, Suite 125, Saint Paul, MN 55101, 651-224-9431, info@jeromefdn.org, www.jeromefdn.org

Amy Lowell Poetry Traveling Scholarship
Boston, Massachusetts

$37,000 travel grant for one year.

APPLICATION DETAILS: Send two copies of either one printed volume and twenty typed pages of your most recent poetry or forty typed pages of poetry, and a signed application letter. Curriculum vitae is optional. The winner will be notified at the end of January, and will receive the first payment before disembarking so as to make travel arrangements. Most winners start their year in September. The deadline is October 15.

This is a scholarship that lifts you, literally, off the map and lands you on an Atlas. It pays you $37,000, in four installments, and stipulates that you travel outside of North America for one year to write poetry, without returning for any reason. It is usually awarded to a poet with at least one book, although the review panel claims that the past publications of applicants is of no consequence.

The Imagist poet and critic Amy Lowell (1874–1925) was born into an aristocratic Massachusetts family that considered poets to be "almost disreputable," despite creating a few. That might have stalled Lowell in her own career, which began when she was twenty-eight, but with a mother who was both a linguist and musician, it could be said that the apple fell close to the tree. Lowell twice traveled outside of North America—to Europe as a girl with her family, and to Egypt for a year as a woman when her fiancé fell in love with someone else. A feisty, entertaining, and generous woman who couldn't spell, she wrote six hundred fifty poems in twenty-three years, had a "Boston marriage" with her Muse, the actress Ada Dwyer Russell, and won, posthumously, the 1926 Pulitzer Prize.

Amy Lowell broke convention and considered herself part of a feminine literary tradition, so it is surprising that past winners include only fourteen women in fifty-three years. They are Elizabeth Bishop, Caroline Finkelstein, Debora Greger, Rika Lesser, Phillis Levin, Elizabeth Macklin, Mary Jo Nealon, Adrienne Rich, Mary Jo Salter, Gjertrude Schnackenberg, Elizabeth Spires, Lynn Sukenick, May Swenson, and Sharon M. Van Sluys. Other winners include Nick Flynn, Richard Foerster, Galway Kinnell, and Mark Wunderlich.

F. Davis Dassori, Esq., Amy Lowell Poetry Traveling Scholarship, Choate, Hall & Stewart, Exchange Place, 53 State St., Boston, MA 02109-2804, 617-248-5253 (speak to Pearl E. Bell, Trust Administrator), Amylowell@choate.com for questions by email, www.amylowell.org to download application.

Money for Women/Barbara Deming Memorial Fund Inc.
Bronx, New York

$1,000 grants to writers of poetry, fiction, and nonfiction.

APPLICATION DETAILS: Send three copies of completed application form, a project description, a budget, a résumé, a twenty-five-page excerpt from work to be funded, and a $10 application fee. The deadlines are June 30 and December 31.

These are project grants open to U.S. or Canadian writers whose work addresses women's concerns or speaks for peace and justice from a feminist perspective. They are awarded twice a year. Barbara Deming (1917–1984) was a feminist, political activist, and writer of poetry, fiction, and nonfiction who came out as a lesbian about a decade before she died of ovarian cancer. Arrested numerous times for her protests against racism and violence, she wrote many books, including *Revolution and Equilibrium*, *We Cannot Live Without Our Lives*, and *A Humming Under My Feet: a book of Travail*.

Susan Plines, Administrator Money for Women/Barbara Deming
Memorial Fund Inc., Grants in Poetry, Fiction, and Nonfiction,
P.O. Box 630125, Bronx, NY 10463

National Endowment for the Arts
Washington, D.C.

$20,000 Literature Fellowships in Poetry and Prose

APPLICATION DETAILS: Send nine copies of a writing sample; see application for details. The submission period is January 3 to March 1.

These fellowships, awarded to twenty individuals each year, pave the way for the recipients to make a name for themselves by setting aside time for writing, research, travel, and general career advancement. The $20,000 Literature Fellowships are available to published creative writers of exceptional talent and awarded in even-numbered years to poets and to fiction and creative nonfiction writers in odd-numbered years. Applicants are eligible if they have published a certain amount of writing with a certain number of publishers in a particular time frame. A full-length book is enough, or in the past seven years, five works of prose in two or more literary journals, anthologies, or periodicals regularly publishing prose, or twenty poems in five or more of these publications.

The National Endowment for the Arts is the largest annual funder of the arts in the United States. An independent federal agency, it is the official arts organization of the United States government and awards more than $100 million annually, with every state represented. The only fellowships granted to individuals are literature, NEA Jazz Masters, and NEA National Heritage Fellowships in the Folk and Traditional Arts.

National Endowment for the Arts, Literature Program, 1100 Pennsylvania Avenue NW, Washington, D.C. 20506, 202-682-5400, webmgr@arts.endow.gov, www.arts.endow.gov

---

"I have never felt more privileged than I did at the American Academy in Berlin. I had a lovely apartment with a splendid view, the meals were exquisite, and the staff could not do enough for you. For me, being on the outskirts of the city was an advantage. Though the heart of Berlin is only a short train ride away, Wannsee itself, where wild boar and fox are often sighted, can seem like the country. I found this quiet, beautiful setting ideal for work. And for fun after work, Berlin can't be beat."

—Sigrid Nunez, author of *The Last of Her Kind*
(Farrar, Straus & Giroux, 2006)

National Science Foundation
Arlington, Virginia

Antarctic Artists & Writers Program travel and provisions for writers, painters, photographers, historians, or scholars of the liberal arts.

APPLICATION DETAILS: You can apply on your own or through an institution; follow the National Science Foundation's proposal guidelines available on their website. The deadline is June 7.

This grant is for the intrepid writer with substantial achievement in arts and letters. Instead of money, winners receive round-trip economy air travel between a U.S. airport and a port of embarkation for the Antarctic—New Zealand or southern South America—travel between there and the Antarctic, a loan of polar clothing, and room, board, and travel in the Antarctic. Six people a year go to research stations, camps, and wilderness areas in Antarctica or get on ships in the Southern Ocean to make observations to complete their projects. Past winners have included Kim Stanley Robinson, Barry Lopez, Gretchen Legler, Donald Finkel, and Jennifer Armstrong. Winners pay for food and lodging during their travel to embarkation points, incidental expenses in Antarctica, and all aspects and costs of completing and distributing the proposed work.

There is no permanent human population in Antarctica, and the people who do live there conduct research or provide operational support. The National Science Foundation funds and manages the U.S. Antarctic Program, which offers the Antarctic Artists & Writers Program. They believe that the science, geography, culture, and politics of this inaccessible landscape is as interesting to those in the intellectual arts as the scientific community. The accomplishments of the winners increase understanding of the Antarctic and help document America's Antarctic heritage.

Antarctic Artists & Writers Program, Office of Polar Programs, Room 755, National Science Foundation, 4201 Wilson Blvd., Arlington VA 22230, ksilverm@nsf.gov or bstone@nsf.gov, www.nsf.gov

New York Foundation for the Arts
New York, New York

$7,000 Artist Fellowships for writers of fiction, nonfiction, poetry, plays/screenplays.

APPLICATION DETAILS: Send completed application forms and four copies of a work sample of ten pages of poetry or twenty pages of prose; artist statement; and résumé. If a written work is an excerpt, you may include a statement that gives the readers context. You can apply in up to two categories each year but can only be awarded a fellowship in one. The fellowship deadline is early October.

The Artist Fellowships for $7,000 are for writers at any stage of their career, who are at least eighteen years of age, and residents of New York State. They are awarded in sixteen artistic disciplines over a two-year period—eight categories a year—and are for unrestricted use. Poetry and nonfiction (2007, 2009, etc.) alternate with fiction and plays/screenplays (2008, 2010, etc.). Poetry includes all forms from the page to the stage; nonfiction includes essays, monographs, criticism, autobiography, journalism, and experimental forms. Since 2001, six of the one hundred forty-two winners are nominated for the $25,000 NYFA Prize by the Artist's Advisory Committee. The winner is selected by the Board of Trustees and awarded the prize during a ceremony in late May. Three writers were among the six nominees in 2005: Mark Bibbins, Melissa Haley, and David H. Surface. Haley, an archivist, won for her essay on "historic boyfriends." Applications are available online in mid-August. Winners are notified in March or April. Recipients must teach a workshop or give a lecture in some part of the New York State community during their year and will not receive the last $700 of their fellowship until they satisfy this requirement.

Founded in 1971, the New York Foundation for the Arts has given more money and support to individual literary, media, visual, music, and performing artists and arts organizations than any other comparable institution in the United States. Their goal is to provide the time and resources for the creative mind and the artistic spirit to think, work, and prosper. Since the artist fellowships began in 1985, NYFA has awarded more than $22 million to more than three thousand five hundred fifty-five artists. In 2005, they awarded one hundred forty-two Fellowships to one hundred forty-three artists, with two of them working in collaboration.

Past winners include Claudette Bakhtiar, Jo Ann Beard, Mermer Blakeslee, Americo Casiano Jr., Xuya Chen, Junot Diaz, Patricia Spears Jones, Bill Kushner, Johanna Lee, Liselle Mei, Nova Ren Suma, Christopher Stackhouse, D.S. Sulaitis, and Chuck Wachtel.

New York Foundation for the Arts, 155 Avenue of the Americas, 14th Floor, New York, NY 10013-1507, 212-366-6900 (tel.), 212-366-1778 (fax), nyfaafp@nyfa.org

Princess Grace Foundation
New York, New York

$7,500 Playwright Fellowship.

APPLICATION DETAILS: Send application form with resume and personal statement. Letter of recommendation is optional. The deadline is March 31.

This fellowship grants an emerging playwright a residency at New Dramatists, and representation and publication by Samuel French, along with a stipend of $7,500.

Princess Grace of Monaco was deeply committed to the performing arts. During her lifetime, she helped many young and aspiring artists realize their dreams of a performing arts career. Following her passing in 1982, HSH Prince Rainier of Monaco and his family established the Princess Grace Foundation–USA as a tribute to Princess Grace and as a way to carry out her legacy.

Princess Grace Awards Playwright Fellowship, 150 East 58th St., 25th Floor, New York, NY 10155, 212-317-1470, www.pgfusa.org

The Puffin Foundation Ltd.
Teaneck, New Jersey

$1,000 to $2,500 grants for emerging artists and arts organizations in the categories of literature, art, music, dance, photography, and theater.

APPLICATION DETAILS: Send a completed application form, project proposal, and work sample. For details, send a #10-sized SASE for application packet. Proposals are accepted from October 1 to December 30.

These project grants are for those who feel excluded from mainstream opportunities due to their race, gender, or social philosophy. The puffin was saved from the brink of extinction in the northeastern United States with the help of concerned citizens. Established in 1983, The Puffin Foundation believes in joining forces with other concerned groups and individuals to ensure that the arts not only survive, but flourish.

The Puffin Foundation Ltd., 20 East Oakdene Ave., Teaneck, NJ 07666, 201-836-8923, www.puffinfoundation.org/grants/ prospectiveapplicant.html

Sigurdur Nordal Institute
Snorri Sturluson Icelandic Fellowships
Reykjavik, Iceland

APPLICATION DETAILS: Send a curriculum vitae and a brief, thorough account of the purpose of your stay in Iceland. The deadline is October 31.

This grant pays travel and living expenses for writers, translators, and scholars in the humanities to stay in Iceland for at least three months to improve their knowledge of the language, culture, and society. A special three-man committee comprising representatives of the

Sigurdur Nordal Institute, the University of Iceland Literary Institute, and the Writers' Association of Iceland awards the fellowships.

The Sigurdur Nordal Institute is a financially independent institute at the University of Iceland, devoted to promote Icelandic culture and history, and to build links between scholars in this field in Iceland and abroad.

Snorri Sturluson Icelandic Fellowships, Sigurdur Nordal Institute, P.O. Box 1220, 122 Reykjavik, Iceland, nordals@hi.is, www.nordals.hi.is

Society of Children's Book Writers & Illustrators
Los Angeles, California

$1,500 Work-in-Progress Grants

APPLICATION DETAILS: Look for guidelines on the society's website in October. The submission period is February 15 to March 15.

These grants are available to members of the society and assist in completing a book project. In any given year, one might apply for General Work-in-Progress grants, for a work whose author has never had a book published. There are four winners in each category and four runners-up for $500.

SCBWI, formed in 1971 by a group of Los Angeles–based writers for children, is the only international organization to offer a variety of services to people who write, illustrate, or share a vital interest in children's literature. The SCBWI acts as a network for the exchange of knowledge among writers, illustrators, editors, publishers, agents, librarians, educators, booksellers, and others involved with literature for young people. There are currently more than nineteen thousand members worldwide, in more than seventy regions, making it the largest children's writing organization in the world.

Society of Children's Book Writers, Work-in-Progress Grants, 8271 Beverly Blvd., Los Angeles, CA 90048, 323-782-1010, scbwi@scbwi.org, www.scbwi.org

Emergency Money

The following organizations offer money to pay for health and other emergencies. If there is a website, only brief details are given. It is best to contact the administrator.

American Society of Journalists and Authors
Writers Emergency Assistance Fund
1501 Broadway, Suite 302
New York, NY 10036
www.asja.org

Authors League Fund

Interest-free Loans
31 East 28th Street, Tenth floor
New York, NY 10016
fax: 212-564-5363
www.authorsleaguefund.org

Carnegie Fund for Authors

Grants-in-Aid Program
1 Old Country Place
Carle Place, NY 11514

PEN American Center

PEN Writers Fund
PEN Fund for Writers and Editors with HIV/AIDS
588 Broadway
New York, NY 10012
212-334-1660
www.pen.org

FINAL WORD

I hope this book has helped open your eyes to the many creative opportunities out there for writers who want to hone their craft. Although obtaining an M.A. or MFA in creative writing, staying at an artists colony, or winning a grant or fellowship would all point you toward a successful career, more important is that each of these experiences offers a way to help you achieve the flow that is essential to good writing. If you can get there, you've made it. If you have flow, you can create whatever literary work you imagine. I hope you will find this essential creative flow, and that I will get to read the evidence one day.

INDEX

Index

Index

Index

ABOUT THE AUTHOR

PHOTO BY BARRY GOLDSTEIN

Amy Holman is a published poet and a literary consultant. She regularly teaches at The New School, Bread Loaf Writers Conference, and Hudson Valley Writers Center, and travels widely to speak at conferences and graduate schools. Her essays on the writing business have appeared in *Poets & Writers* magazine and *AWP JobLetter*, and her poetry won the Dream Horse Press National Chapbook Competition and was selected for *The Best American Poetry 1999*. She lives in Brooklyn, New York.